ULTIMATE
PREY

MERRY CHRISTMAS
NANCY.
THANK YOU FOR
EVERYTHING
YOU DO!
LOVE Sal
12/23

ULTIMATE PREY

The True Story Behind
The Yosemite Sightseer Murders

Stephen M. Sanzeri

SMS & Associates, San Francisco

ULTIMATE PREY

Copyright © 2012 by Stephen M. Sanzeri

Published in the United States by SMS & Associates
San Francisco, California.
smsanzeri@gmail.com

ISBN 978-0-9859144-0-0

Author, Stephen M. Sanzeri

Cover & Design by Stephen M. Sanzeri

Edited by Suza Lambert Bowser

Printed in the United States of America

First Edition

For

Carole, Juli, Silvina and Joie

CONTENTS

CONTENTS

ULTIMATE PREY

THE TRUE STORY BEHIND
THE YOSEMITE SIGHTSEER MURDERS

PROLOGUE

Cary Stayner was found guilty for the Yosemite Sightseer Murders, but most people closely associated with the investigation believe that Stayner did not act alone. Law enforcement had the right guys from the beginning, so what in the hell happened?

For five years, Stephen Sanzeri, former police officer, private investigator, and bounty hunter, investigated the tragic deaths of Carole Sund, her daughter, Juli Sund, and their friend, Silvina Pelosso. The answers he found were startling.

Now, for the first time, the real story is finally being told.

The criminals who committed these crimes with Cary Stayner have not been punished. Some remain in prison on unrelated charges and some are still at large.

For this reason, I have changed many of the names in the book. Other than this, everything that I write here is the truth as I found it.

Stephen M. Sanzeri

INTRODUCTION

Prior to my current job as a private investigator, I was a cop, a bail bondsman, and a bounty hunter.

I was the guy who cleaned up other peoples' messes. My success rate was about ninety-nine percent. I'd get phone calls from kiss-ass bail bondsmen about to lose thousands of dollars. I'd get what was known as "dog" cases; these were shit cases because there was almost no time left on the bond.

Dog cases were tough. Usually, the fugitives had been on the run for months. I was the cleanup hitter. You can bet it's a lot harder and way more dangerous chasing bad guys that have evaded capture for a long time. It means they had help and that makes the whole process a lot more dangerous. Call me an adrenaline junkie, but I have to admit, I dug the action.

The bail bonding agencies that hired me were also my competition. Even though they got a little hot and bothered when they needed to hire a competitor to find their fugitives, they knew who to call.

Then came along a bounty hunt that led me to Alabama and into one of the most dangerous chases of my life. I was pursuing the killer of three innocent women. The case became known as the "Yosemite Sightseer Murders." I never could have been prepared for the hellish world I walked into.

And it has haunted me ever since.

"There's nothing more challenging, unpredictable or more dangerous than the hunting of another human being."

Ernest Hemingway

CHAPTER 1

June 7, 1999
Fultondale, Alabama

"MANHUNT"

THE MANHUNT FOR fugitive, Paul Candler Jr. was in full swing. The slippery bastard had eluded me twice. I wanted Candler in the worst way, and it wasn't just for skipping out on a felony gun possession warrant. I was sure he was dirty for murder. In fact, I was convinced he was involved in more than one brutal killing.

It was about an hour before sunrise. My partner, Rick Janes, and I, were standing on the side of Alabama Highway 131, itching to join the Jefferson County Deputies, Fultondale and Birmingham Police Officers. These guys were about to comb the swamps, searching for my fugitive, Paul Candler Jr.

There wasn't much traffic at dawn on Alabama Highway 131, but Rick had a hunch. And when my partner's instincts spoke up, I listened.

"Do you want to split up?" Rick said. "It would be faster."

"Too dangerous," I said.

We started walking down the highway.

CHAPTER 2

November 23, 1998 – 7 Months Earlier
Murphys, California

"THE BAIL"

SHE WORE A long black overcoat and black high heels. Her hair was long and bottle brilliant. Her tan was store-bought with a little too much orange; Calaveras County doesn't boast a lot of sun in November.

"May I sit?" she asked.

"Sure," I said. And so she did, and she made a show of it, slowly crossing her nicely shaped bare legs.

"It's a little wet out there," she said. "I should have dressed warmer."

"Been raining cats and dogs since this morning," I said. "But since this is Calaveras County, I guess I should say 'frogs'."

She smiled, but I don't think she got it.

"You Mr. Sanzeri of Sanzeri Bail Bonds?"

"Call me, Steve."

She looked about 42-years-old, but was probably a few years past that. Not half-bad, she was obviously a broad who took care of herself

"What brings you to my office, Ms.?"

"Dobbins . . . Barbara Dobbins."

"I take it you need a bail bond."

"My old man went in last night."

"What's his name?" I said.

"Paul Candler," Barbara said. She placed her hands on her knee, displaying blood red nail polish and a large rock on her finger.

It looked like Barbara Dobbins had a little money or she liked to flash like she did. Her skirt length would have bought her a spanking or a weekend dishwashing at St. Agnes Catholic School for girls. She was flirting with me and I didn't mind.

"What did Paul Candler do?" I asked, enjoying the show.

"He didn't do a thing. Those cops are always harassing him."

"Maybe," I said, "but something happened to get him arrested."

"He's in Sonora at the county jail. He was arrested for drunk driving and having a gun. That was all."

"A gun!" I said. "What kind of gun?"

"A pistol of some kind," Barbara said defensively. "I don't know; I don't know shit about guns."

"Does he carry a gun all the time?" I asked.

"Sure, most of the time. Come on, Steve, lots of people carry guns and they don't go to jail for it." She stroked her knee suggestively and looked at me with big sky blue eyes. "Well, are you going to help me or not?"

I smiled at her little act. "How much is your boyfriend's bond?"

"Twenty-five thousand, and I can get it."

"Really?" I asked.

She purred and smiled, while I thought it over. Gun charges are risky bails no matter what the circumstances are. On the flipside, they are usually higher bonds and sometimes worth the risk for the money. I explained to Barbara the cost for the bail bond premium and amount of collateral.

"I need ten-percent for the bail premium. That's twenty-five hundred. The collateral to secure the bond has to be at least ten grand, and I need that in cash," I said.

"Why do I need to pay the collateral?" Barbara pouted. "Ten-thousand's a lot of money to come up with."

I took another peek at that rock. "You said you could get the money."

"I can," she said, crossing her arms, annoyed.

"Listen to me. If Paul misses his court appearance, and I don't get him before a judge in six months, the full amount of the bail is due. Twenty-five thousand puts me in the poorhouse, Ms. Dobbins. You'll get the collateral back if Paul doesn't jump bond on me. There's no problem as long as Paul makes it to court."

"Paul won't go anywhere. He'd never leave me!"

I've heard that line before. I wasn't betting the farm that this bail would fly. Twelve-thousand and change, is not easy to come by, but judging from the stone on her finger, I felt optimistic and phoned the Tuolumne County jail.

Katrina, the booking clerk confirmed the misdemeanor drunk

driving charge. However, the gun charge was felon with a firearm, a serious felony. Candler had a long rap sheet; he'd done hard time.

Barbara was looking out the window at the rain.

"Where did Paul do state time?" I asked.

"What?" Barbara turning her long, slow gaze my way.

"Prison time," I said, "what did he do time for?"

"I don't know. Some sort of bullshit. He hit some guy in a bar, up in Groveland."

"Really," I said.

"That's what I was told."

"Let me enlighten you," I said. "How about felony assault, controlled substance, sexual assault, assault on a peace officer? He's a real cookie, Barbara." I paused. "You sure you want to get him out?"

For a moment, her eyes were clouded with confusion...or was it fear?

"I can get the money," Barbara said shivering.

I've seen this look a few times. Women with 'issues' look like this. They're the ones that hook up with real shit birds; men who beat them and share drugs. I think it's called codependency with a capital "C." Hmmm, I thought, this might not turn out to be an easy deal.

Paul Leckey Candler Jr. had a long criminal history that included years in the joint. Even though I was having second thoughts, I knew business was slow.

I was talking myself into the deal. I reminded myself that most of the ex-cons I bailed out have never jumped bond. In fact, most don't. They know the system and understand the consequences.

Deciding to go for it, I shook hands with Barbara Dobbins and she split to get the money.

Two hours later, she arrived back in my office. Still wet but dressed now in tight jeans, she counted out the cash. Water dripped from her hair onto the bills. She looked over at me.

"You got something I can dry myself with?" Barbara asked, looking at my shirt meaningfully.

"Will tissues do?" I handed Barbara the box. She plucked a couple out and dabbed at her face. Then, she looked at me with that flirty smile. I smiled back at her. She was kind of sexy, but I was more interested in the cash.

"Thanks, almost done," Barbara said, as she counted out the stacks of bills.

I thought about all the bills I could pay.

"Please," I said. "Take your time."

CHAPTER 3

November 23, 1998
Sonora, California

"A BAD FEELING"

I MET BARBARA Dobbins at the Tuolumne County jail that afternoon at 3:00 pm. She was out front, smoking a cigarette. I walked up to her.

"Any time," I said.

Barbara took two more drags and then butted the cigarette in the cement ashtray next to the door. I led Barbara into the deserted lobby. I reminded her again that I was taking a big risk posting this bond for her boyfriend.

Candler was a habitual criminal who'd probably end up back in the joint. I've stepped into this territory before. Sometimes, it comes with a few sleepless nights, but like I said, business was slow.

"Thanks for doing this," Barbara said. "I talked to three other bail companies and none would help. They saw Paul as a bad risk."

"He is," I said. "Just make sure he makes all of his court appearances. If I have to chase him, you might need to pawn that rock on your finger."

Barbara smirked and gave me the evil eye. I wondered if that ring was worth more to her than Candler. Looking back, maybe I should have proposed that rock as some extra collateral.

But, for ten-thousand in cash, I thought I could chase Paul Candler to the limits and make a few bucks at that.

Bounty fees are expensive. I get a hundred and seventy-five dollars an hour and that's per man on my team. When I need Rick along, the cash collateral pays our travel expenses, too.

About an hour had passed since I posted the bond with the clerk, and I noticed that Barbara was getting anxious.

"How much longer, Steve?"

"Soon."

I was about to give her a better answer, when the crashing sound of the opening jail door boomed through the lobby. Then, Candler

6

made his appearance.

The first things I noticed were the tattoos on both arms. Jailhouse "tats" began at his wrists and ran up to his beefed out biceps, also called "sleeves." Most of them were Peckerwood and Aryan tattoos, some of the most dangerous prison gangs in the country. The prison tats referred to white power affiliations, whose recreational activities of choice usually included crystal meth and whooping on minorities.

Candler's black short sleeved shirt looked a size too small, probably a purposeful choice designed to add to his tough image.

Candler was about my height, 5'10," but thirty pounds lighter than my 210 pounds. He was in good shape and looked like he could handle himself.

I approached him, but he ignored me to smack a lip-lock onto Barbara, as if he hadn't seen her in months. I waited a short minute.

Bored with the performance that was probably for my benefit, I said, "Hey! Candler! I'm Steve Sanzeri, your bail agent."

Candler ignored my voice and moved his hands around Barbara's waist, gazing into her eyes.

"Thanks!" He grunted without looking at me.

"You're welcome," I said sarcastically. This guy was already getting on my nerves. "I need you to fill out some paperwork, and . . ."

"Give me a minute." He interrupted as he stroked Barbara's ass.

Fuck his minute, I thought, feeling more and more pissed off.

"Come on, baby," Barbara said soothingly. "Let's get this done," she dropped her voice to a fake whisper, "so we can go home and fuck."

Barbara slipped one last tongue into Candler's mouth, then, she turned and gave me a look as if to say, *"Don't you wish this was you?"*

Why they wanted to share their sex talk with me was a question that demanded too much information. Shit, I didn't really want to know.

Finally, Candler turned and looked at me full on. What I saw gave me a chill: although he was smiling, his eyes were flat and metallic. They reminded me of rat eyes. I saw them for what they were: the cold, merciless eyes of a predator . . . feral and inhuman.

CHAPTER 4

June 7, 1999
Fultondale, Alabama

"WE FOUND HIM"

THE MEMORY OF those merciless eyes haunted me as Rick and I walked along Alabama Highway 131, seven months later. Candler had jumped bond and we were hot on his trail. We checked out four motels and struck out each time. Finally, we entered the lobby of a Motel-6. A young black woman was busy vacuuming the lobby.

"Good morning," she said pleasantly as she turned off the machine.

"We're looking for a guy," Rick said.

Frowning slightly, she said, "Police already been by. Yo man ain't here."

"How do you know that," I asked, Miss...?"

She must have liked my face, because she smiled at me and said, "Call me Maxine. I'm the night manager. The police came by earlier and spoke to Brian."

"And Brian is?" I asked.

"Ya'll ain't from 'round here, are ya?" Maxine asked and ran her fingers over her flat-ironed hair.

"No, ma'am," I smiled back encouragingly. "We're from California."

Maxine's eyes widened. I could see her thinking about California. Maybe she was fantasizing about Disneyland or dreaming of a place filled with movie stars.

I waited patiently while she collected herself. She looked down at the vacuum cleaner handle in her hand and said, "Brian's the day manager. He say he didn't see the guy. He say nobody done checked-in that looked like the man the police are lookin' for."

"Maxine, do you have a copy of that wanted poster?" Rick asked.

Maybe she was a little flustered by all the California attention or maybe it was my shining personality. Anyway, she smiled distractedly and gestured at the desk.

I leaned over the counter and spotted the poster on a pile of copy paper. I held it up so she could see Paul Leckey Candler's ugly mug.

"What do you think?" I asked.

Maxine examined the wanted poster with curiosity.

"Hmmm. I ain't never really looked at it," Maxine said, "And I ain't never talked to the cops neither."

"Is he familiar?" I said.

"Oh my!" She exclaimed. "He sure do look familiar."

"Maxine," I said. "Why don't you check the register for "Dave Geer." She walked around behind the counter and clicked on the computer. She frowned a little as she read the screen. Then, she looked back at the poster.

"Oh my!" Maxine said again. She put her hand over her mouth.

"What is it Maxine?" Rick said.

"That's him," she said. Maxine trembled, horrified that a criminal might be staying in her motel.

"Take it easy Maxine," Rick said, "you're safe."

"Oh, my Lord! I remember him! He looked strange; he was all wet. Why, he smelt just like the dang swamp!"

"What room is he in?" I asked. For a moment she simply stared at me as if she couldn't understand what I was saying.

"Maxine, what room?" I asked her again. But, I could see that she was reading the bottom of the poster, the part about Candler being a person of interest in the Yosemite murders.

She looked at me with horror in her eyes.

She was speechless.

CHAPTER 5

February 14, 1999
Yosemite National Park

"MISSING"

STANDING IN THAT Motel-6, while Maxine tried to regain her voice, I knew she was flashing back to what had made headlines in the national news at Yosemite National Park, one of the most famous places in the world.

It was back in February 1999, right around Valentine's Day, when this American symbol of natural beauty and serenity changed forever with the disappearances of 42-year-old Carole Sund, her 15-year-old daughter, Juli, and their young Argentinian friend, Silvina Pelosso, sixteen.

The trio had departed Eureka, California, on February 13, in a rented red Pontiac Grand Prix en route to Yosemite National Park. They stopped in Stockton, California where Juli participated in the American Spirit Association cheerleading.

After the competition, Carole, Juli and Silvina continued south where they stayed the night in the farming town of Merced, about an hour south of Yosemite Park.

Back in Eureka, Carole's husband Jens, and their other three children Jonah, Gina and Jimmy, prepared for their trip to meet up with Carole and the girls on Tuesday, February 16, at the San Francisco International Airport.

Juli was thinking about attending the University of the Pacific, so, Carole planned on leaving Yosemite early that same day to take a tour of the campus and then onto the Bay Area.

Juli would then fly home, and Silvina would continue to travel with the Sunds to Arizona to experience another wonder of the world, The Grand Canyon.

Carole and the girls pulled into the tiny town of El Portal (650 pop.) in the midafternoon on February 14, Valentine's Day, where a

10

room awaited them at the Cedar Lodge, about five miles west of Yosemite National Park. It had been a harsh winter, and there were very few guests staying at the lodge. Of the lodge's 210 rooms, only a dozen or so were occupied.

Strangely, Carole and the girls would be staying alone - the only tenants in the rear building.

The following morning, Carole, Juli and Silvina headed off for a sightseeing trip into Yosemite Park. With fresh snow on the ground, they tossed snowballs, ice skated and took goofy pictures of each other having fun. It was Silvina's first time in the snow, and Carole wanted to make sure Silvina was enjoying herself.

Late afternoon, the cold set in, and the skies darkened. Carol and the girls went back to their room where hot showers awaited. Then, they walked to the hotel's empty restaurant for burgers, fries, and shakes.

After reminiscing about the day's adventures, laughing and making plans for the next morning, Carole paid the bill and they walked back to room 509, leaving Carole's veggie burger to-go, forgotten on the counter.

They were never seen alive again.

CHAPTER 6

February 19, 1999
Murphys, California

"BAD NEWS"

IT WAS AROUND 10:15 a.m. and I was in my office talking with my bounty hunting partner, Rick Janes. The television was at a low volume in the background, and we were discussing my pending bail skips as well as the PI cases Rick was working.

"When you get some time, I could use a hand," Rick said.

"What do ya have going?" I asked.

"Remember that pipe bomb case out of Amador County that you posted bond for?"

"Sure do," I said. "I think the guy's innocent as hell."

"Might be," Rick said.

"And?"

"I caught the defense case and I need some interviews done."

"Conflict of interest, partner," I said. "I'm his bail bondsman."

"I'll take my chances," Rick said. We both paused a moment as we noticed the local news on the TV. The headlines were all about the three women who had disappeared from Yosemite.

Rick sighed, "Damn. That's bad. What do you think?"

"Probably a car accident," I said. "You know how dangerous the roads are around Mariposa. Hell, wet or dry, cars are always going over a fucking cliff off forty-nine."

"Yeah," Rick said hesitantly. "I don't know. Feels kind of weird to me."

Rick left for a lunch date to meet up with his wife, Kathy. That reminded me of the growling sound coming from my stomach; I was getting hungry.

I opened the foil wrapped burrito on my desk as I swiveled my chair toward the television and listened.

"After Mariposa County Sheriff's Deputies and Park Police searched miles between Yosemite Park and Mariposa, with the initial suspicion that the three women sightseers may have wandered off a hiking path and gotten lost, or driven off an icy road and down a cliff; there are new developments . . ."

I turned up the volume.

" . . . The billfold of Carole Sund's wallet was found by a pedestrian along a busy intersection in Modesto, and police now believe that foul play may be involved with the disappearance of the Yosemite sightseers."

I looked at the Valentine's card on my desk from a former girlfriend. Shit, I thought. If those women had disappeared, they'd never get another Valentine. Ever.

I didn't know then, as I devoured my noon burrito, how a bail I had posted nine months earlier would lead me into the case of the Yosemite Sightseer Murders.

CHAPTER 7

February 20, 1999
Modesto, California

"CRAZY DAY"

SATURDAY AFTERNOON, RICK and I were en route to Modesto for a bounty.

"Let's stop and get something to eat," I said, "a snack to hold us over."

"Sounds good," Rick said. "I need a pit-stop anyway." Rick went to take care of his business, while I shopped for a Coke, some cashews, and a Heath Bar.

While I was waiting, I checked out the *Modesto Bee* newspaper displayed in front of the counter. The cover story was about the missing women in Yosemite. The big news was that Carole Sund's billfold was found the day before right here in Modesto. I bought a copy.

"Would you like a bag, sir?" the clerk asked.

"Sure, thanks," I said.

Rick showed up with a bottle of water, milk, and some peanuts. We got into the van and munched our snacks.

"What are you reading?" Rick said.

"I'm checking out the Yosemite case." Then, I turned to page two, where I noticed another local story.

"Missing Skier at Bear Valley." Wow, I thought, another disappearance so close to home? Odd. Bear Valley is only about 35 miles from my house and even closer to Rick's.

"Hmmm," I mumbled.

"What?" Rick said.

"Did you hear anything about a doctor missing up at Mt. Reba, Bear Valley?" I said.

"No, nothing, what happened."

"It says that Doctor Katherine Wong, a pediatrician from Santa Clara, was reported missing while skiing with her family at Mt. Reba."

"Right in our backyard," Rick said.

"Yeah. Weird."

"Some people don't pay attention, Steve. They ignore the signs and end up off a trail. They get lost, trapped in the snow."

"Yeah, it happens." I said. But I felt a strange feeling in the pit of my stomach: four women disappearing in less than a week. Something was strange.

Rick and I searched for our bail jumper until 9:30 that evening, with no luck. It was our first attempt, and I had plenty of time left on the bond.

We headed home through the valley, and the air was foggy pea soup. The 120 minute drive from Modesto to Calaveras County is dangerous enough without fog.

I actually felt relieved that we didn't have a prisoner on board. These guys can turn into pains-in-the-ass real quick. With the driving conditions that evening, I needed all the concentration I could muster to focus on the road.

I was making a sharp turn in the "soup," when my cell phone rang.

"Yeah!"

"Steve?" the caller asked.

"Yeah, this is Steve, who's this?"

"Paul Candler."

"What can I do for you, Paul?"

"The cops are chasing me, man. They think I burned down my sister's house."

"No shit," I said.

"They came by my house, and I split."

"Where?" I asked.

"Doesn't matter."

"The fuck it doesn't matter! You're out on bail, man, and my ass is on the line."

"You're supposed to help me, Sanzeri! Call Barbara. You remember her? My girlfriend? The one who gave you all that cash?"

"Yeah, yeah. I remember. Where's she at?" I asked.

"Out in La Grange, at her ex-husband's place."

"Where are you?"

"I'm at Chinese Camp, at a phone booth. If they arrest me, you gotta fuck'n bail me out. You gotta call my chick."

"Look, Candler, I'm on the road. If something happens, and they hook you up, have Barbara call me. Meanwhile, it might really help if you tried to stay out of trouble!"

"Shit!" Candler said. "I gotta go."

Rick had been listening, of course. "Who was that?" Rick asked.

"Future prey!"

"Who is he?"

"Do you remember that scumbag, Paul Candler, the Aryan asshole I bailed out of Tuolumne County for a deuce and felony firearm charge?"

"Sure do," Rick said. "That was him?"

I explained to Rick that the call was strange, but so was Paul Candler. He was a tweaker — a meth freak — probably loaded like a rat. It was totally possible that he might have torched his sister's place. When I had the time, I'd look into it.

Then I remembered his cold stare — those flat, feral eyes. My gut instinct told me that I was going to see Candler again, and it wasn't going to be pretty.

After dropping off my partner, I headed home. Walking in the door, I turned on eleven o'clock news. The FBI announced that they had joined in the search for the missing sightseers.

I didn't put it together until much later, but the fact that Candler had called me only 4 days after the women went missing was significant. This was just one aspect of a series of events that led me into the murder investigation.

Another component was the fact that local law enforcement had said very little about the disappearance of Dr. Katherine Wong. The fact that Dr. Wong had vanished into thin air, combined with the tweaked-out phone call from Candler, and the ongoing search for the missing women from Yosemite stayed with me during the night.

My sleep was restless, and the dreams I could remember were filled with ugly images – the kind you don't want to remember.

CHAPTER 8

February 25, 1999
Mariposa County, California

"IT'S GETTING DANGEROUS"

THE YOSEMITE DISAPPEARANCES were getting to me. Sure, bad things happen: accidents, car crashes, overdoses, burglaries, but violent crimes are more common in urban areas.

Hell, that's why a lot of us live in the country: to get away from shit like that. Like many proud Americans, who live near Yosemite, I consider this incredibly beautiful monument to be a safe place for people to visit. Now, all that had changed.

The Feds were all over the case. For two weeks, every available law enforcement agency pounded the pavement, following every possible lead. Search and rescue teams from Mariposa, Tuolumne, Calaveras County and surrounding agencies worked 24/7 in a 30 mile radius around the park and failed to find the red Pontiac Grand Prix or any sign of Carole and the girls. Sacramento FBI Special Agent in Charge, James Maddock told the press, *"We feel almost certain that the women were victims of a violent crime."*

The Carringtons' (Carole's parents) immediately offered a $250,000.00 reward. It seemed obvious that the Carringtons' had access to money; kidnapping for ransom crossed my mind as a motive. Law enforcement had probably thought that, too.

Over the next two weeks the FBI, along with every law enforcement agency within six counties, including the State of California's Department of Justice, began tracking hundreds of leads. The publicity from the Carringtons' reward produced a lot of phone calls, but it was the news media that birthed the majority of them . . . maybe too many. Investigators could not follow up fast enough as the story headlined every news organization in the nation.

Then, it seemed like there was a break. On March 5, 1999, two people of interest were arrested for parole violations and possible connections to the case.

The first to get his ass hauled in was Billy Joe Strange, a 39-year-old resident of El Portal, a small town 14 miles west of Yosemite Village.

Strange — yeah, great name! — was a parolee who worked at the Cedar Lodge lounge and restaurant. A felon with past convictions and prison time for rape, drugs, and attempted murder. The FBI and state parole agents yanked Mr. Strange's parole for possession of a knife, a "no-no" while having a parole tail.

Billy Joe Strange fit his name as well as the profile of a sex offender and violent felon—just what the FBI was targeting in the sightseer disappearances.

The second dirt-bag to get picked up was Eugene "Rufus" Dykes, a 32-year-old felon with past convictions for statutory rapes, drug charges, felony assaults, and weapons charges.

Dykes was arrested after a short standoff with police and parole agents in Modesto, California. Loaded on meth, Dykes surrendered without incident and was sent back to state prison the following day.

Then, on March 14, Darrell Gray Stephens, Billy Joe Strange's roommate, was rolled up for failing to register as a sex offender. Convicted back in 1978 for rape and robbery, Darrell Stephens was also questioned about the missing sightseers.

It looked as though law enforcement was doing a good job shaking-down the local bad guys, but Carole, Juli and Silvina were still missing. Pressure from the victims' families and the media were beginning to weigh heavily on the investigation. It had been a month since the girls were last seen alive.

On the evening of March 18, 1999, investigators found themselves up against another person of interest. Michael "Mick" Larwick, a 42-year-old armed felon, shot Officer Steve Silva in the guts – twice, during a routine traffic stop. Over 30 rounds of ammo were exchanged. In an effort to get away, Larwick commandeered a home in Modesto and held off law enforcement for 14 hours before being gassed out and arrested.

Yeah, Mick was quite a guy. His past activities included: stabbing a rival boyfriend eleven times in the back for sleeping with

18

his girlfriend and kidnapping and raping his former sister-in-law in front of her children.

"Mick" Larwick was part of a vagabond group of methamphetamine drug users and dealers that were centered in the Modesto area, which stretched through small towns on a corridor only a two hours distance from Yosemite.

The "Modesto Cranksters" had quite a reputation, and, like any small rural area, you can bet on one thing: everybody knows everybody, especially in those circles.

The FBI questioned Larwick for hours about the sightseers' disappearance. With a long criminal history including prison sentences for rape, drugs, firearm convictions, and attempted murder, Larwick looked like a good candidate.

His father, Leroy Larwick, was a Bigfoot theorist, and he'd gained quite a reputation for supposedly spotting Bigfoot in Tuolumne County. Leroy lived up near the Long Barn, where Mick spent his formative years, learning to become a tweaker. Long Barn – a town that would later become very important in the case.

In another twist, Larwick was the older half-brother of Eugene "Rufus" Dykes. Nothing like keeping up a family tradition of drugs, rape, sexual molestation, and firearm violations.

This case was close to home and local news was all over it. I was impressed with the aggressiveness of law enforcement. They were focusing on the right group of people.

I'd been a bail agent and bounty hunter for seven years, and the Mother Lode and California's central valley were part of my turf. I was familiar with the criminal underground and knew many of the players.

I thought the FBI was heading in the right direction, and just as things were starting to look up, with more parole sweeps and probation violations around the corner, the Carrington, Sund, and Pelosso families' worst fears were confirmed.

On March 18, the same day that Michael Larwick was arrested, Tuolumne County resident, Jim Porter, was hiking alone just outside of the small town of Long Barn, almost three hours from Yosemite Village. Hidden in the trees on Wheeler Road, just off Highway 108, Porter discovered a burned up car.

The car was a red Pontiac Grand Prix.

The FBI and investigators arrived and opened the trunk. Inside, there were two charred bodies burnt beyond recognition. They covered the sad sight with a large tarp and transported it to the local Columbia Airport.

What was once the rental for a fun holiday was now evidence in at least two homicides. The blackened dirt and melted snow that outlined the car was a crime scene.

Within a few days, both bodies were identified through forensics and dental records. It was Carole Sund and Silvina Pelosso. My heart dropped when I heard the news and I wasn't alone. I think everyone in the nation was in shock.

But where was Juli Sund?

Location of *Carole Sund* & *Silvina Pelosso's* Bodies & Routes the Killers' Drove

Murder Victims' Location

Map is not to Scale

Drawn by Stephen M. Sanzeri

CHAPTER 9

March 19, 1999
Murphys, California

"HE FUCKING JUMPED BOND"

THERE WERE A shit-load of ex-cons and violent felons living in and around Sonora, Jamestown, and Calaveras County. Over the years, I've posted bonds for some of the worst. Naturally, I was curious if any of my people may have been involved in the murders.

It was March 19, 1999, the day after Carole Sund's and Silvina Pelosso's bodies were found. I stopped by the post office after running errands. I received the usual junk mail and some bills, and court forfeiture from Tuolumne County Superior Court. As I walked to the car, I opened a half sealed envelope, and, there it was: the forfeiture for Paul Candler.

Shit, I thought, that figures. I hustled to the office and pulled Candler's file. I didn't have a lot of forfeitures, maybe six or seven. I wanted to get on top of Candler's ass right away. It had only been six days since he missed his court appearance, and the trail was as hot as it was going to be. I called in my partner, Rick.

"Well, man, you thought he would skip," Rick said. "You didn't like Candler from the get-go. Anything about the fire at his place?"

"Damn, I forgot all about it," I said. "I'll call Tuolumne County Fire Department. They may have something."

"When do you want to start after Candler?" Rick asked.

"Soon."

I phoned the Tuolumne County Fire Department. They had no record of a blaze in Moccasin, but the California Department of Forestry, did.

"The fire on February 20, 1999, at 55784 Grizzly Road in Moccasin, is of unknown origin. Only the kitchen area and attached garage wall were damaged. That's all I can tell you, sir," the dispatcher informed me.

Candler wasn't lying; there had been a fire at his house. But, why did he run from deputies unless it was a meth lab that exploded. Or, I thought, with images of a burned up red Pontiac Grand Prix lingering in my mind - maybe another crime was being covered up. Either way, the fire meant something and I was certain it wasn't good. What was he hiding? Candler had no warrants at the time.

I spent the next several days making phone calls and tracking down dead-end leads on my latest fugitive and his girlfriend, Barbara Dobbins.

Their phone number was disconnected two days after I posted Paul's bond; what a surprise! All I had to go on was his last residence on Grizzly Road in the town of Moccasin, about 40 minutes from Long Barn, where the red Pontiac was found.

I thought of Candler, the missing women, his strange phone call on February 20th – four days after the women disappeared - the physical proximity of the car, and the timing.

A cold chill ran down my spine.

CHAPTER 10

March 25, 1999
Murphys, California

"TOO CLOSE TO HOME"

ABOUT A WEEK later, I was getting ready to hit the sack. It had been a grueling day, because I was preparing to move on Candler's bond forfeiture – something that takes a lot of legwork and organization. I was beat, but I wanted to catch the ten o'clock news.

The opening story was no surprise, but there was a new development. The FBI announced that a girl's body was found in Tuolumne County. I felt sick. It had to be Juli Sund.

They found her corpse on a hillside above Lake Don Pedro, near the town of Moccasin, about halfway between Yosemite Village and Long Barn. The same scumbags that had murdered this young woman must have stashed the Grand Prix, containing the bodies of her mother and her friend, near Long Barn.

Transporting and stashing bodies is a lot of work. Driving hours from Yosemite to do it told me that several people had to be involved.

Like everyone else, I'd prayed that Juli would be found alive. But, after her mother and Silvina were murdered, I expected the worse. Who would kidnap and brutally kill these women?

I was disturbed, and I couldn't sleep. I put on a shirt and drove to my office.

What fucking savages could kill three innocent women? I pulled the files of clients that had convictions for rape, drugs, assault, and murder. I was looking for bails I wrote in Tuolumne, Calaveras, and Stanislaus Counties. I had a feeling that I was about to uncover something.

Not surprisingly, there was a bunch that looked pretty good to me. I narrowed it down to those who lived closest to Lake Don Pedro at the Mariposa and Tuolumne County border, and one person stood out: Paul Candler Jr.

His last residence on Grizzly Road was a stone's throw from

Lake Don Pedro, less than two hundred yards from the water.

PAUL LECKEY CANDLER JR.

I called my partner.

"Rick," I said, "did you see the news?"

"Sure did. Unbelievable. Pretty close to home."

"That's why I'm calling. Our next bounty might be for a murder suspect. This is no coincidence, Rick. I think Paul Candler might be involved."

"You think?" Rick said.

"I do," I said. "Remember the phone call in Modesto when he torched his sister's home? Then he jumps bond?"

"Yeah, I remember."

"Well, check this out: Basically, he lives on the fucking lake."

I paused and took a breath. "I don't think he's running just on my bond. He took off just *before* the bodies were found."

Rick and I talked until a quarter to one in the morning. I had our plan worked out, and we would be on the road by 8:00 a.m.

When I hung up, I thought of those rat eyes. I knew if Candler and I came head-to-head, one of us was going to get hurt.

The bond on Paul Candler was my responsibility, twenty-five thousand dollars of responsibility. I had no choice but to find him.

The cops might get him first, but there was no guarantee of that.

As far as I knew, investigators hadn't linked Candler to the murders. As for me, the writing was on the wall and I couldn't ignore it.

Candler had jumped my bond. His last residence was very close to Juli Sund's body. The Pontiac and the charred bodies of Carole and Silvina were discovered over the hill off Highway 108, above Sonora, about 40 minutes from the Grizzly Road address.

Candler's criminal history definitely upped his stock. We would be handling this bounty like a manhunt for a murder suspect.

As far as I was concerned, there were no rules when three women are murdered.

I wasn't a cop anymore. The bad guys didn't play fair. I'd be tossing out the rulebook on this one.

It was crunch time. I was up early with very little sleep. I pulled the shotgun and extra ammo from the safe. I had the TV turned up waiting for the early news.

"The FBI announced early this morning that they are looking into a *"loose knit gang of meth freaks' that frequent the central valley and foothills,"* the reporter said.

At around 8:00 a.m., I met Rick and his wife, Kathy, at my office. I hadn't thought much about Kathy joining the bounty, but it wasn't a bad idea. Kathy was a former police officer and always welcome on a hunt. I never turn down an extra gun, especially on a bounty hunt like this.

We discussed plans for our trip to the town of Moccasin. Located at the Mariposa-Tuolumne County line, on Highways 49 and 120. Moccasin is about as small and rural as it gets.

We arrived in the area about 40 minutes later, but before heading to Candler's home on Grizzly Road, I decided to detour and take a look at the rest stop off of Highway 49, just above where Juli's body was discovered at Lake Don Pedro.

As I drove up the short hill to the parking area, we noticed a black undercover unit that was occupied with two official looking guys in black suits. There was a third man standing close to the car and smoking a cigarette. There were also three news station satellite vans parked nearby. A quick turn around and we left.

"Looks like Feds," I said.

"Yeah," Rick said grimly. It was best to stay stealth for now.

There was no reason for anyone to know what we were up to. The undercover guys were definitely FBI. The vehicles and suits gave that away. We started up the road after Paul Candler.

"Should only be a mile or so from here," Rick said. "A left turn at the top." We traveled slowly down a steep gravel road with our eyes peeled for Candler's house. This place was rural; there were not a lot of homes around.

"Where do you think it's at?" I asked.

"Can't tell," Rick said. "No numbers out here."

"Look for a place that caught fire," I said.

We stopped at the bottom of Grizzly Road, which dead ended to a boat ramp on Lake Don Pedro. The 13 or so homes we passed were all off road at least 200 feet or so. I turned around and we made another pass.

"I still can't see anything," Rick said. "Pull over and let's walk the road."

I needed a stretch anyhow. Rick scanned below with his binoculars as we stood on the road's edge.

"There's something down there," Rick said. "I think that blue house could be it."

"Let me see," I said. I looked through Rick's binoculars.

"I see it," I said. "Don't see signs of any fire."

"Look at the back of the garage, see it?" Rick said.

"Um . . . yup! You're right."

"See the furniture next to the garage," Rick said, "looks like it caught fire."

"That's it," I said. "Jesus Christ."

"What?" Rick said.

"Rick, it's only a quarter mile from where Juli was found. Just across the water; unbelievable."

I looked at Kathy. She stared back at me, shock in her eyes. Rick's face was serious. We all realized how close Paul Candler Jr. lived to where Juli Sund's body had been found.

After watching the house for a few minutes we concluded that it was vacant. The gravel driveway hadn't been used for a while. Candler wasn't around.

We had no other leads, so over the next few weeks, we took several trips to Sonora, Jamestown, Long Barn, Twain Harte,

Greenville, Miwok Village, Groveland and Tuolumne City.

Nobody had seen Paul Candler or Barbara Dobbins. I spoke to Barbara's stepdaughter in Jamestown, but she was short with me. She was pissed-off for some reason, and she hadn't seen her stepmother in months.

As for the Yosemite Sightseer Case, the investigation was at full throttle. The FBI, investigators, parole agents and probation officers were shaking down meth dealers and addicts, violent felons, sexual predators, and there were plenty to choose from.

Scumbags in the central valley and Mother Lode had never been so actively targeted as individuals or as a group. Law enforcement agencies kicked doors all over the place, initiating parole and probation searches on every felon that fit the profile, within 30 miles of Tuolumne and Mariposa Counties.

I felt the repercussions of the criminal roundups. Pressure from investigators caused my informants to get sudden lockjaw or a bad case of amnesia. Basically, my snitch wire was shutdown.

They were scared, and I couldn't blame them. The Grand Jury was preparing indictments, and a few of my snitches would probably be subpoenaed as witnesses.

Guilty or innocent, a few of them knew who committed the Yosemite murders.

Location of *Juli Sund's* Body & Routes the Killers' Drove

Murder Victim's Location

Map is not to Scale

Drawn by Stephen M. Sanzeri

29

CHAPTER 11

April 6, 1999
Modesto, California

"COLLATERAL DAMAGE"

PAUL CANDLER WAS a player in the central valley and Mother Lode methamphetamine trade. He also knew many of the suspects who were under investigation. Now, Candler was on the run. Why?

One answer was easy: when law enforcement turns up the heat, the area's doper population goes underground. Witnesses get scared. And, then, people start to disappear. Yeah, they disappear or…they get killed.

The first major collateral damage involved a murder. Terry Ray was a material witness in the Yosemite Murders Case and just about to testify before the Grand Jury in Fresno, California.

He never got the chance.

On April 6, 1999, his body was discovered floating in the Stanislaus River, boots and all. Terry Ray was a known associate of Michael "Mick" Larwick, and also a member of the central valley "meth club."

It was starting to get messy. Anyone who got in the way was going to have problems or end up dead, like Terry Ray.

During the first week of April, the Grand Jury in Fresno subpoenaed those who'd been apprehended on suspicion or who were potential witnesses in the murder case. Besides the now-deceased Terry Ray, the Grand Jury focused on Eugene "Rufus" Dykes, and his half-brother, Michael "Mick" Larwick.

The FBI seemed confident that the half-brothers were involved. Michael Larwick grew up in Long Barn, in Tuolumne County, not very far from Wheeler Road, where the red Pontiac was discovered.

It didn't take much to figure that only a local would know where to hide and torch a vehicle so flames and smoke wouldn't be noticed. Larwick was a crazed desperado. He'd just shot Officer Silva twice in the stomach, trying to evade capture.

My mind kept asking why?

30

As for Eugene Dykes, there were pink blanket fibers discovered on Juli Sund's body that closely matched fibers found on Eugene Dykes' jacket. There were also matching fibers inside his Jeep Cherokee, now in police custody.

And then, there was Eugene Dykes' initial confession to investigators after he was arrested. That's right. Eugene Dykes confessed to his involvement in the murders of Carole, Juli and Silvina.

There's a lot of sociological study about false confessions. Sure, guys confess to crimes they didn't commit to avoid other charges. But, in this case, it was hard to ignore Dykes' confession.

The interview by the FBI, and Stanislaus County investigators was not video or audio recorded.

I couldn't believe it! Apparently, investigators were not prepared for Dykes to "spill the beans."

A second interview with Eugene Dykes was videotaped and this time Dykes held back information he had stated earlier, but said enough to incriminate himself in the murders.

Apparently, Dykes was high as a kite when he first confessed. The second time, he was sober. I guess that made him change his story real quick and he laughed about it!

Dykes even bragged to his cronies about leading the FBI around by the nose, visiting places that he hinted might have been important locations, telling them that he couldn't remember. Maybe here, maybe there. "I ain't sure."

After several days of Grand Jury testimony, no indictments were handed down. Insufficient evidence against Michael Larwick and Eugene Dykes dropped these dopers to the bottom of the suspect list.

Investigators found fibers matching those found on Juli Sund's body in Dykes' Jeep Cherokee, in Mick Larwick's Corvette, and on Dykes' San Jose Sharks jacket. But, by the time, Dykes had led investigators around in circles; this evidence seemed to lose importance. And I couldn't understand why.

The majority of the Grand Jury's witnesses were associates of the half-brothers. But nobody wanted to go up against these bad boys.

One witness already swam with the fishes. No way in hell were any dopers going to testify.

I kept wondering where Candler was in all of this. His name was never mentioned before the Grand Jury.

The Yosemite Murder investigation was beginning to stall.

Meanwhile, where was Paul Candler?

CHAPTER 12

May 27, 1999
Sonora, California

"OUT OF LEADS"

I FORWARDED A 12 page report to the FBI's taskforce "Tour Nap," in Sonora, outlining my investigation of Paul Candler Jr. I proposed that the investigators take a hard look at my fugitive.

There were too many coincidences not to consider Candler a suspect or at least someone closely connected or complicit in the murders.

Rick and I spent a lot of time on this bounty. We had no idea where Candler or Barbara were holed up. Candler was a career criminal, and Barbara was a good looking con artist. Both were street smart and could survive almost anywhere.

I had plenty of time left on the bond, and it was rare for me not to catch up with a fugitive, especially with the amount of time we'd spent on this bounty.

This case was eating at me. I was neglecting other business because of Candler, and if something didn't pop soon, I was going to have to shift gears. On the other hand, I felt like I couldn't let it go. I liked Paul Candler as a suspect in the Yosemite homicides and that was motivating enough for me to keep on his ass.

I had more aggressive tactics in mind. Up to this point, I'd been fairly lax and busted no balls. Felons and dopers were my eyes and ears, and a lot of them owed me favors.

I also never burned my snitches, so I had a pretty good relationship with the underground. I wanted to collect on my markers, but pressuring informants was not in the cards. They were getting enough heat from cops.

Breaks come and go, and I was due for one soon. Word was out about Paul Candler and Barbara Dobbins. My phone might ring at any time; and it did. But, it wasn't from any of my snitches or from the FBI taskforce. It was much better.

CHAPTER 13

June 4, 1999
Jamestown, California

"THE PHONE CALL"

ONE OF MY strategies is to befriend my enemies' - enemies. In other words, I keep the enemies of my enemies close at hand; find out who hates who. Become buddies with those guys.

Getting close to people that despised Candler or Barbara Dobbins wasn't difficult with the trail of shit they left behind. This included Barbara's estranged stepdaughter, Anne.

When the phone rang, I was surprised to find Anne on the other end.

"I appreciate the phone call, Anne," I said. "But you were really short with me last time. In fact, you were downright rude."

"I know, I'm sorry. To tell you the truth, I didn't want to talk." She hesitated. "Paul scares me."

"I can't blame you, Anne. He's one scary guy."

She was silent for a moment, hesitating. I was patient; it felt like she might have something for me.

Finally, she spoke, "Steve, they're in Alabama."

I sat up straight in my chair. This was the break I'd been waiting for.

"Are you kidding me?" I asked carefully.

"No, I'm dead serious, and she's with Paul," Anne said.

"How do you know this?"

"Barbara called this morning, and I wrote down the phone number from the caller ID."

"You spoke to Barbara?" I said.

"Yeah," Then, she added bitterly. "She owes me money. Anyway, you want the info or not?"

"Is the Pope Catholic?"

I got the phone number, checked the area code, and cross-reference. The number came from the Sumiton, Alabama area and belonged to Sumiton Mobile Home Sales. I guessed that Barbara worked there, or at the least, had borrowed the phone. Either way, Alabama was a long way to run.

No wonder I couldn't find Candler. And why Alabama? Using a weak southern drawl, I phoned and asked for "Barbara."

"Hello, ma'am, my name is George, and I was there last week looking at one of those…uh…mobile homes, one of the big-uns. I talked with a red-haired lady. She had bright red hair, and she was real nice."

"Hi George, my name's Macy. That's probably Barbara. She's at lunch right now. May I take a message sir?"

"No, Miss Macy, that's all right," I said. "How's about I just call back later?"

"Why, yes, sir. You betcha! Barbara will be back at one o'clock."

"Oh, and ma'am, I had one more question?"

"Yes, sir?

"Barbara sure seemed to know what she was doing. You musta trained her real good. How long she been working for ya'll?" I asked.

"Barbara has only been with us for a little over a month," Macy said. "She came from California. We think she's doing a good job."

Bingo! This was a huge break! There was no reason to wait. I phoned Rick.

"Pack your bags, partner. I found him."

"No kidding!" Rick said. "Where we going?"

"Alabama, you been there?" I asked.

"Nope," Rick said.

"Neither have I. We leave on the red-eye tonight out of Sacramento. I'll pick you up at nine."

"I'll be ready," Rick said.

My clothes and gear were packed and ready. I cleared my handgun, retrieved extra magazines and ammo, and then I took a satisfying shot of single malt Scotch.

I realized this was it. Hell, I'd had a bad feeling about Candler's bond from the beginning.

And what about Alabama? Nobody from California runs to fucking Alabama. Paul Candler was running from a lot more than my bond and a year in the joint.

I contacted the Tuolumne County District Attorney's Office and informed them of my plans for Alabama. Not only was it their warrant for Paul Candler, they were one of the primary investigating agencies in the Yosemite case.

The D.A.'s office agreed to extradite Paul Candler after his arrest, but didn't express any interest in what I had to say about their fugitive's relationship to the Yosemite case. In fact, like so many short-sighted law enforcement agencies, they were caught up with their public image and their own agenda. They didn't give a rat's ass about what I had to say.

"I can't believe it, Rick," I said, as we were flying over Salt Lake City.

Believe what?" Rick asked.

"The Tuolumne Deputy D.A. didn't give a shit about what I had to say about Candler."

"Well, you sent a report to the FBI, and you never heard back from them, either," Rick said. "Shit, they know what happened in Mariposa; they don't want you involved. You might make them look bad. They know all about you. They know what we're doing. Believe me partner, they're watching."

Jesus Christ, the Mariposa Mess was back to haunt me. Rick was one-hundred percent right.

"You think they know about Candler?" I said.

"Probably a lot more than you know."

CHAPTER 14

June 6, 1999
Birmingham, Alabama

"CHASE BEGINS"

OUR PLANE LANDED at the Birmingham airport just before 2:00 a.m. We picked up a rental van and headed south toward Sumiton, Alabama.

Forty minutes later, we were in town, and looking for the Sumiton Mobile Home Sales.

"That wasn't a bad drive," I said.

"No, not bad," Rick said. "Isn't the mobile home lot supposed to be on the highway?" Rick asked.

"Somewhere along here. Should be easy to find.

At the airport, I'd picked up a Sumiton newspaper with a couple of intriguing headlines: "Woman in Bathing Suit Accused of Stealing Sumiton City Tractor; "Python Still on the Loose." I couldn't pass those up!

The kicker is that they were two separate stories, and both were true. Sumiton might be a rural Southern town, but it sounded like there was plenty of action. I only hoped my Bounty action would be quick and easy.

As we came over a small rise—Sumiton's pretty flat—we noticed several mobile home lots on both sides of the highway.

"Jesus, these things are popular around here," Rick said.

"You know the old saying about Alabama divorces and tornadoes, don't ya?" I waited a beat. "Somebody's going to lose a trailer!"

Rick laughed.

"Which one says Sumiton Mobile Home Sales?" I asked.

"I'm looking . . . there it is. The last one on the right."

I moved over a lane and slowed down. The place was well lighted, gated like a fortress.

"Who the hell is going to steal one of those?" I said.

"Nobody," Rick said. "The security's for vandalism and vagrants...they sleep in them."

"Maybe Paul and Barbara live in one," I said. "Something to consider when thinking about interrupting the cozy Candler couple."

There was an old abandoned gas station across the highway that would be good for surveillance. Our plan was to follow Barbara home after work. That should take us to our target, Paul Candler.

Feeling pretty good about the plan, we found a motel and crashed for the rest of the night.

It's standard practice to notify local law enforcement whenever we bounty hunt in a different jurisdiction. So, after a late breakfast, we went to the Walker County Sheriff's Department around noon to check in.

Outside the Sheriff's Office, we paused for a moment when we looked at City Hall across the street. A huge Confederate flag flew proudly above the courthouse. We were speechless.

A young black deputy came out of the Sheriff's Office, and we asked him if a supervisor was available. He looked like a rookie, about 24-years-old. He directed us to the right door and was about to split, but stopped when I asked my partner about the City Hall building across the street.

"Say, partner, what do you make of the Confederate flag over there? What kind of bullshit is that?

"Kind of strange," Rick said.

The deputy stood by politely, then he said, "This must be ya'lls first time down here."

I stared at him. "I'm sorry, but isn't flying that flag frowned upon nowadays?"

The black deputy looked at us and shook his head in disbelief. "You askin' me?"

He smiled with bitter amusement. "Good luck, fellas." Then, he walked away, staring up at the flag across the street and shaking his head.

This wasn't my first time in the South. I'd spent some time in Atlanta and Louisiana, but I'd never seen the Confederate flag displayed over a government building.

"How can I help you gentlemen?" desk Sergeant Yancey asked as we entered the lobby.

"We're bail enforcement agents from California, and we believe

38

our fugitive is in your town," I said.

Rick opened the folder and handed the file to the sergeant.

"Nice looking fella," Yancey commented cynically, examining Candler's hard-bitten mug. "What do ya'll want him for?"

"He jumped bond for drunk driving and a firearm beef," I said. "He has a felony warrant in NCIC."

"Is that right?" Yancey scratched his head.

"Sure is," Rick said. "We also believe he's involved in the Yosemite Murders."

The sergeant looked up from the wanted poster at Rick. "What did you say?"

"We think our guy is involved in the Yosemite murder case," Rick repeated.

"I know about that case," Sergeant Yancey said. "Those poor girls. Alabama is a long way to come. Ya'll really think your guy is here?"

"Oh yeah, we know he is," I said.

We explained our plans to the sergeant, and he agreed to lend us whatever help he could.

"You know fellas, we don't take kind to out-of-state white trash from California, much less this close to home. Just holler and we'll back ya'll up. We always have room to exit one more piece of shit."

As a rule, we always receive good cooperation from agencies out of state and this was no exception. The cops like getting rid of vermin that's not native to their turf.

"Did you see the sergeant's eyes light-up when I mentioned the Yosemite case?" Rick said.

"I don't think we're going to have any problems down here," I said.

We headed toward Sumiton Mobile Home Sales. It was close to one in the afternoon and the humidity was bad. It felt like we were wading through water, our shirts slick on our backs.

"I'm gonna turn up the air," Rick said.

"Go ahead," I said. "It's fucking humid as hell."

"What kind of car is Barbara driving?" Rick asked.

"No idea, but, if one has California plates, chances are it's hers."

I knew what Candler drove: a beat-to-shit blue 4-wheel drive Toyota pickup, and an older, green Ford pickup. I had no clue about

Barbara's ride.

"There's the gas station," Rick said.

"Got it," I said.

"Go around the back." He slurped a Coke. "Let's get the layout of the place."

I circled the building and parked in front, where I saw a couple of antique 'out of service' gas pumps. The island's overhang was intact—a welcome addition to our surveillance.

"Can you see the front of the office?" I said.

"Sure can . . . hey, wait a minute, back up a few feet," Rick said.

"What is it?"

"I think I see a car with California plates."

There were seven or eight cars in front. I looked through my binoculars.

"I see it," I said. "It's a red Toyota Celica. That's got to be Barbara's."

We had a few hours before game time. Barbara would get off work late afternoon, and, then, we would follow her back to our bad guy. Everything was going as planned.

Then, a deep male voice came from my side of the van.

"You boys know ya'll are trespassing?" the man said.

I sat up and looked at the side view mirror. The red and black plaid shirt was a blur.

"What in the hell are you doing on my property?" the man said, as he stood next to the van, a .45 auto in his right hand.

"I'm sorry, sir," I said. "We're watching for a fugitive."

"What kind of fugitive?"

I showed him my badge. Rick's arm crossed my chest as he held out his.

"We're bounty hunters from California, sir," I said.

"Anybody's got a fuck'n badge. Show me some paperwork!"

I handed the man a copy of the wanted poster.

"A real sweetheart!" he exclaimed as he squinted. "Them's some serious eyes . . . you boys armed?"

I nodded.

"Yes sir," Rick said.

"That's good," the man said approvingly. "Well, I own this joint, and I wish ya'll asked me first." He spat out a stream of tobacco. "My name's Lavelle Roberts."

40

Rick and I got out and introduced ourselves.

"We're sorry, Mr. Roberts," I said. "Your place looked vacant."

"Well, it ain't." He gestured at the sign over the defunct gas pumps. "See the sign?"

I looked at a peeling picture of a parakeet nailed to the wall.

"I sell birds, bird feed, and cages. Haven't pumped a gallon of gas since '83. Opened this place in '46 after I came home from the War."

There've been plenty of wars; I was glad I knew which one he meant.

Lavelle Roberts looked at his watch and peered across the highway. A leather faced man, with tobacco stained hands, Lavelle was in his late sixties. He was short, about five-foot-seven, but in pretty good shape. This veteran of the Second World War was a character, an old goat that would have no problem taking on King Kong.

Mr. Lavelle Roberts was all right with me.

"She usually leaves around five-fifteen, or so," Lavelle said.

"Who?" I said. "Are you talking about Candler's girlfriend, Barbara?"

"Noticed her the first time she drove up," he said. "California license plates. Ya don't see many around these parts."

Lavelle spat a long stream of tobacco onto the dirt. "I've seen that Candler guy pick her up sometimes. I recognize him from your wanted poster. Looks like a real fuck'n piece of work. She's only been working there a month or so. So tell me, what's the crime you want this fella far?"

"Besides our bounty, felon with a firearm," I said, pausing, "Murder."

"Murder?" Lavelle said.

"Mr. Roberts . . ." I said.

"Call me Lavelle."

"Lavelle, do you know about the Yosemite murders in California?" I said.

"Sure, I know 'bout Yosemite. I been there. You fellas looking for the killers of those poor girls?"

"Yup!" Rick said.

"You think it's this fella you're chasing; he's the killer?" Lavelle said.

"There's a good chance he's involved," Rick said.

"Well boys, you can park here long as you need to. How's about a beer or some iced tea?"

Nice. We had a concealed spot, out of the blazing sun, with an unobstructed view of Sumiton Mobile Home Sales and the red Toyota.

Lavelle brought us a couple of patio chairs and some iced tea. He had a few beers and sat with us the entire time with his 12 gauge Winchester shotgun just an arm's length away next to the screen door.

Whatever made him feel comfortable was OK by me. Hell, it was his gas station, his state, and, probably, his militia.

There wasn't much going on around the mobile home lot. A couple of cars in, a couple of cars out. I was bored and hot.

"Lavelle," I said, I wouldn't mind a beer, your next trip in."
Rick looked at me.

"You want one?" I said, knowing the answer.

"No thanks," Rick said, looking away.

"Here ya go," Lavelle said, "a cold one and some more peanuts."

I teased Rick with the ice-cold beer; he was not amused and wiped the sweat off his face with his sleeve.

"You boys know 'bout us here in Walker County?" Lavelle asked.

"Sure don't, Lavelle," I said.

"We're the hit capital of the United States." Lavelle said. "We were on *60 Minutes* last year. It put us on the map!"

I looked at Rick, and he gestured with a shrug. Lavelle was smiling.

"Hit capital as in . . . Hit?" I said.

"You got it," Lavelle said. "We're the place to come for hired hits. Like the TV show said, people come down here, if they want somebody taken care of."

He shot another long stream of brown juice. "I got some men, ya know? This fella that you boys are chasing, you want us to grab him?"

"That's O.K., Lavelle," I smiled, impressed. "We've got it handled."

"Thanks for the offer," Rick said, "but we need him alive for

Steve to get off the bond."

"O.K.," Lavelle said, "only takes one call, if you boys change your minds. I'm going to get another beer. Want one?"

"No thanks, I'm good."

I knew exactly where Lavelle was going with this. I remembered a television special on *60 Minutes* about Walker County, Alabama. I guess that murder for hire is as common as bass fishing down here.

Lavelle liked us and we liked him. And that was just fine. But, I didn't need the "Militia," even though Lavelle Roberts was a card-carrying member.

This train of thought carried me to Candler. Why was he hanging out in the "hit" capital of the country?

I looked at Rick, "What the hell is Candler doing here?"

"Maybe he's got family down here, or Barbara does," Rick said.

"No, I checked all of that. Did you hear what Lavelle was saying?"

Rick paused, thinking it over. "You're thinking Candler is a hired gun."

"Maybe," I said, wiping my face.

"Yeah, he's a bad ass," Rick said, "but that might be taking it a little too far."

"But, not out of the question," I said. "Remember, we're not just chasing him because of the bounty."

Man, it was hot. I pulled my drenched shirt away from my skin; it didn't help.

I thought about Candler's pending felony charges and his criminal record. It wasn't out of line to think he had a notch or two on his gun belt.

Rick and I believed that Candler had a hand in the Yosemite slayings. Why not get paid to kill, if it's something you do anyway. Maybe Paul Candler moved here to start a new career.

It was close to five o'clock when Lavelle walked up with his gun in hand.

"It's time for my supper," Lavelle scooped tobacco out of his mouth and threw it on the ground. "You boys got my number. Ya'll just give me a call if you need me."

We watched Lavelle walk away. I noticed he had a distinct limp. Must be a war wound, I thought. I looked at my watch. "Should be anytime," I said.

"Should be," Rick said.

"We need to grab him fast," I said, watching Lavelle close his screen door. "I don't want a lynching before we can get Candler out of town."

It might be what Candler deserved, but that wasn't my call.

CHAPTER 15

June 6, 1999
Fultondale, Alabama

"SO FAR SO GOOD"

STAKE OUTS DEMAND patience, but I was starting to run out. Just then, Rick raised his binoculars and stared across the highway.

He let out a breath. "Jesus, that's the reddest hair I've ever seen. Can't be real."

"That's her," I said, spotting Barbara getting into the Celica. I was as excited as a kid on Christmas morning. Finally! I get to open the presents. I pulled onto the highway, as Barbara tore off down the road.

"Man, she's driving like a bat out of hell!" I said.

"She's heading for Birmingham," Rick said.

"Looks like she's in a hurry."

"Back-off a little and see if she slows up."

I pulled way back. After about five miles, Barbara made a left turn onto a one-lane country road.

"What in the hell are they doing way out here?" I asked.

"Good place to hide," Rick commented.

We passed a sign: "Welcome To Warrior, Population 120," I read the sign out loud, as we passed it.

"Welcome to Mayberry," Rick said, "the perfect hideout."

The place was pretty and as innocent as Aunt Bea's apple pie: green fields, white picket fences, large front yards, ranch style homes. Looked like there were more horses than cars or people.

"She's still driving like Mario Andretti. It's a neighborhood, for God's sake!" I said.

"How fast?"

"Fifty . . . fifty-five, she's flying."

"It's twenty-five, here," I said. "Think she made us?"

"Maybe!"

We were in a minivan and Barbara was driving a small car. If she wanted to lose us, she could. Keeping our "rabbit" in sight and staying under 50 miles per hour was a chore. Then, we attracted some unwanted attention.

"Did you see the cop?" Rick asked.

"Shit," I said. "What cop?"

Rick looked in his side mirror, and, then, turned his head to the rear. "Better slow down partner."

If we got stopped we would lose Barbara, so I slowed to forty.

"Oh, man. He's right behind us." Rick said.

"I don't see Barbara," I said. "Shit!"

There were no speed limit signs or at least I didn't see any. My guess was that twenty-five to thirty mph was the maximum limit. If the deputy got me on radar I was done.

"I can't fucking believe this," I said.

I pulled to the right, trying to avoid a deep drainage ditch, and stopped.

"We lost her, Rick," I said.

"Let's see what happens. The town isn't that big."

The deputy crossed to the passenger side of the van. Rick's window was down, and I could hear the gravel crunching as the deputy approached.

"Afternoon, boys," the deputy said, as he leaned into the car.

"Good afternoon," Rick said.

"Ya'll in a hurry?" he asked.

"No sir, I mean, yes, we are in a hurry," I said.

"That's right, deputy," Rick said. "We're following a fugitive's girlfriend. She was in the red Toyota Celica in front of us."

"What in the hell are ya'll talking about?" the deputy asked.

"I'm sorry," Rick said, "we're bail recovery agents from California."

"Ya'll must be them bounty hunters!" the deputy exclaimed. "What do you say you show me a driver's license and both your ID's?"

If there was a model for southern born cops, this guy was the poster child. He sported a military haircut and a pressed uniform with a badge that could be used as a mirror. And he wasn't tiny, either.

Satisfied with our ID's, he said, "I know all 'bout you boys. " In roll-call, they told us you were in town."

He handed us our ID's and licenses. "Listen up, you went through that school zone pretty fast, but school is out and, since there are no kids running around, I won't cite you."

He straightened up and added, "Make sure you call us if ya'll need some help."

"Thank you," I said.

"We sure appreciate that, deputy," Rick said.

"Just keep it under fifty," deputy said, as he turned and walked back to his patrol car.

Barbara was not in sight.

"Where do you think she went?" Rick said.

"No telling, I'll keep going straight."

As I slowed for a stop sign, Rick noticed a small red car parked behind the general store across from a gas station.

"Wait a second," Rick said, "slow down."

"What do ya have?" I said.

"I see the car," Rick said. "Pull over."

"She must have stopped for some smokes," I said. "Same plate?"

"Yup!" Rick said. "I guess we're lucky she has such a bad habit."

Barbara walked out of the store and into her car. We were back in the race. She took off like a bat out of hell.

"Man, she drives fast," Rick said.

"Yeah, but we aren't going to lose her again. We just got a free pass."

Since the turnoff into Warrior, we'd travelled about three miles. Barbara slowed down for a stop sign, but didn't stop. Then, she pulled over to the right, and parked in front of a small green house. I slowed to a crawl. We were about a hundred yards or so behind.

"Must be the place," I said.

"Who's that standing in front?" Rick asked.

"Can't tell for sure, but it looks like Candler."

I stopped by the side of the road.

"I can't see. The bushes are in the way," Rick said.

"I can see. Hand me the glasses," I demanded impatiently. "It's Candler! Hot damn!"

Paul Candler was shirtless and leaning into the car, talking to Barbara. Every few seconds, he would pop-up and look around.

O.K., we found him, now what? In a normal situation, we'd do a drive-by for confirmed ID. But, we had him. Shit. No reason for a drive by, but a turn around would be suspicious.

"Roll up your window," I said.

"Are we driving by?" Rick asked.

"Yeah," I said. "He doesn't know what you look like. I'll turn away. Just get a quick layout of the place. See if he's armed."

We passed the little green house and the Toyota.

"See him, Rick?"

"He looked right at me. Couldn't see if he had a weapon."

"It's a good bet," I said.

I paused for the stop sign at the end of the block. There was a restaurant across the street with a phone booth. We would be out of view and only a quarter of a mile away.

"You weren't kidding," Rick said, "Candler's got a lot of jailhouse tats. Those on his chest are Aryan for sure."

It was time to call in the Cavalry.

"Hey Rick, got some change?"

I made the call, and after a brief conversation with the Walker County dispatcher, a deputy named Bates arrived 20 minutes later, but it was only to deliver a letdown speech.

"We can't do a thing," Deputy Bates said. "Your guy's in Jefferson County. Sorry, not our jurisdiction."

"Where's the county line?" Rick asked. Bates pointed across the street, "Right there."

"Great," I said. "Just about runs through Candler's front yard."

Deputy Bates radioed his dispatcher, and, soon, a Jefferson County unit met with us.

A tall boney man stepped toward us. "Sergeant McNally," he said, shaking hands. "What's up?"

I handed him our folder with the info on Candler.

"So you found him, huh?"

"We have," I said. "Seems like you know all about our guy."

"Word spreads fast in these parts," Sergeant McNally said.

"He's just down the street," Rick said.

"Well," he said, tapping the folder. "Good news? Your boy's in our county. Bad news? We can't help you."

"You gotta be kidding," I swiped my forehead in frustration.

"Apparently, Mr. Candler is not in NCIC," Sergeant McNally

said.

"Sure he is," I said. "I checked with the Tuolumne County Sheriff's Office before we left."

"Sergeant, there's no way we'd be here without a good warrant," Rick said.

"I don't know what to tell you," Sergeant McNally said, squinting against the setting sun. "Unless you get your guy into the National Criminal Information Center, I can't help you. I'm truly sorry, boys. Your guy sounds like a bad one, but we need an abstract from the county that holds the warrant."

"Tuolumne," I clarified.

"O.K., call Tuolumne, get this guy into NCIC, and we'll lend a hand."

Sergeant McNally looked through Candler's file. "Felony firearms charge, hm."

"He's been a regular in the joint," Rick said.

"Yeah, a bunch of times," I added. "They retired his number from San Quentin."

Sergeant McNally looked at us, grinned apologetically, and walked away. His hands were tied, and I was pissed.

I dropped a dime to the Tuolumne Deputy District Attorney's Office. It was Saturday, but there's a 24-hour number for emergencies, and this was urgent.

"They should have an on-call Deputy D.A. available," Rick said. "Most counties do."

"They fucking better," I said, as the operator answered.

"Tuolumne County District Attorney's Office. How may I direct your call?"

"Bill Carlson, please," I said, as I explained the reason for my phone call.

"Mr. Carlson will be right with you," the operator replied, as she put me on hold. It seemed like forever. I started to fume. Finally, he picked up.

"Steve, Bill Carlson, here. I understand you have Paul Candler located in Alabama?" There was a lot of background noise.

"Bill, I can hardly hear you," I shouted. "It's about the warrant."

"Golfing!" Bill yelled back.

"What?"

"I'm in the clubhouse, wait . . ." I waited, tapping on the scrungy phone booth window. He came back on, "O.K., I'm outside. Go ahead."

"We've located Candler in Warrior, Alabama. He's standing in front of his house as we speak."

"Can you grab him?" Bill said.

"He's two blocks away," I said, "but that's not the problem. There's no NCIC hit."

"Sure there is, I checked."

"Bill, the fucking warrant is not in NCIC. Walker County S.O. just checked. I'm out of luck getting back-up until Candler's in the system."

"Grab him and call me back," Bill said.

"No, I don't think so, Bill," I said, "That's not how we roll. We need back up."

"Are you sure it's him?" Bill said.

"One-hundred percent."

"Alabama," he mused. "I didn't think he'd go that far."

"I told you guys that I had him located in Alabama!" I exclaimed, my aggravation growing. "I need this taken care of now. Scratch your golf game and help me out."

"One more question," Bill said. "How did you find him so fast?"

"It's what I do, Bill," I muttered. My irritation must have been obvious.

"O.K., Steve, don't get riled up. I'll see what I can do. It'll take a couple of hours, maybe by midnight." I started to object, but he interrupted me. "I gotta go. Good luck, man." He hung up.

I walked back to Rick, who was slurping down another Coke.

"What did the D.A. say?" Rick asked, tossing the empty cup into the garbage. I put on my sunglasses and headed for the van, feeling irritation swelling in every cell.

"We're on our own."

CHAPTER 16

June 6, 1999
Warrior, Alabama

"WHAT WAS I THINKING?"

MAYBE IT WAS Carlson's casual and unhelpful attitude, maybe it was my frustration, combined with the steamy Alabama heat. But, mostly it was the thought of all the people who ended up hurt or maybe even dead at the hands of Paul Candler.

As I walked to the van, I thought of the unsolved Yosemite Murders; it had been almost four months since the ruthless killings.

I'd sized-up Candler, when I posted his bond. I knew I could take him. But, I really didn't want to move on him without back up. It would either go textbook or go totally "south" on us.

By the time I started the van, I'd made up my mind. Cops or not, I couldn't pass on the opportunity to grab him. Shit! He was standing right there not a quarter mile away!

"I can't believe it's going to take that long to enter a warrant," Rick said. "I entered plenty of warrants in my day. NCIC, an hour, maybe two. Carlson was bullshitting you."

"Either way, Rick, I've made a decision. You with me?"

"You wanna drive by the house?"

Rick asked.

"It's the only way I know out of here," I said.

"I don't think it's a good idea."

"It's been over an hour. He's probably inside."

I turned around in the parking lot and onto the main road. My heart was pounding. It was less than 30 seconds to Candler's place. I pulled to the side of the road to talk it out with Rick.

"This could be our only chance," I said. "We're driving by the house. If he's still outside, I want his ass. If he's inside, it's way sketchy without back up. But, if he's still outside, I say we take him. You with me?"

Rick grinned with confidence. "I'm with you, but let's make it fast," he said, unstrapping his weapon.

"All right," I said, putting the van in gear.

"And we do it only if he's out front." Rick added, "I'm not fuck'n chasing him into the house or through the woods."

Rick rarely cusses. It means he's serious and on his game.

"O.K., man," I said. "Here we go."

Slowly, I got back on the road. The house was a hundred yards away. My stomach tightened.

"Shit, there he is," Rick said.

"She's still in the car!" I exclaimed, surprised.

It was as if they'd never moved. Candler still stood shirtless on the passenger side; Barbara was behind the wheel. I drove past.

"He spotted us!" Rick said.

"Hold on, I'm turning around." Just past the green house, I flipped a fast U-turn. With the noise from the gravel the spinning tires, there was no way Candler didn't know something was up.

I hit the brakes and the van slid to a stop about 40 feet from the car.

Rick was out behind his door with his weapon pointed at Candler. I jumped out.

"Paul! Let me see your hands, now!" Rick commanded.

Candler froze for a split second and, then...un-fucking-believable...he dove head first through the passenger side of the car. Spinning out and fishtailing, Barbara gunned the Toyota onto the road.

I heard her tires squealing. I hit the gas.

"Fuck'n-shit," I shouted. "Dammit!"

"Just stay on her ass," Rick said, fastening his seat belt.

I pushed the van at top speed around sharp turns and over bumps, catching air at 70 miles an hour. After a few minutes it was getting ridiculous.

High-speed chases are sexy on TV. In real life, rolling a van at a high speed can get you or, even worse, some civilian dead real fast. And that ain't sexy.

"Steve!" Rick shouted over the roar of the engine, "Hey, man, we gotta back off!"

"God damn it!" I muttered. I slammed the steering wheel with the flat of my hand, pissed. But, I slowed down. Rick was right.

I slid my foot off the pedal and coasted to a crawl. Paul and

Barbara were out of sight, and I was out of my mind. What was I thinking?

I don't make bad calls very often, but this was a big one, maybe the worst ever. I was not happy with myself.

"Boy, did I screw the pooch on this one, Rick."

"Hey, man, no sweat," Rick said, looking over at me. "It was a good opportunity. I'd do it again."

"Candler sure knows we're after him now," I said, wiping my face on my shirtsleeve. "It's going to be hell trying to find him."

"No doubt," Rick said.

"We chased the rabbit out of its hole. He won't be going home for a while, and he won't stop running until he's caught or killed."

"Or, worse, kills somebody else," Rick added grimly. "I have a feeling we'll get another shot at him."

I hoped Rick was right. We had an extremely dangerous felon on the loose, running from what might also include a triple murder beef.

We'd tipped our hand. Candler knew we were onto him; he'd be more prepared than ever.

I turned the van toward our motel, knowing that Candler had a tremendous advantage.

CHAPTER 17

June 6, 1999
Sumiton, Alabama

"ONLY OPTION"

BACK IN OUR ROOM, after wolfing down a few cheeseburgers, Rick and I discussed our options. It didn't take a rocket scientist to see that these were obviously limited. I still had no word about the warrant, and I wasn't eager to try for Candler again without backup.

"The only thing we have is the house, and he won't be hanging around there now." I said.

"Probably swimming in the swamp with the rest of the snakes," Rick said, tossing down some fries.

I drained a cold beer and finished off my fries. The air conditioning, the food, and a beer had settled me down after a day of disappointment.

"I don't see anything we can do right now." I burped and wiped my mouth. "The warrant still hasn't been entered into the system as far as we know. I guess we just need to wait."

Rick crumpled the dinner remains and tossed them in the garbage. I thought for a minute.

"You know, Rick, I'm not so sure the warrant *wasn't* entered. I don't trust Carlson. He knew I was going to Alabama, and look what the fuck happened."

"Let's call Jefferson County and have them run NCIC," Rick said.

"O.K.," I said. "But, first, I'm headed for a shower." I peeled off my shirt. "I gotta wash off this Alabama sludge."

I stood under a generous stream of water, getting my body temperature under control. Man, that cool water felt good.

Rick stuck his head around the bathroom door and hollered at me. "Hey, I say we hit the house, and squeeze Barbara."

"Say again!" I yelled over the shower noise.

"I think we should talk to Barbara," Rick said.

"Are you nuts?" I turned the water off and grabbed a towel.

"She might give him up," Rick said.

"You're nuts," I said, wrapping the towel around my waist and walking back into the room. "She's been with the fucker for six years. He beats her, they kiss and make up, they share dope, they fight, they kiss and make up. You know, sick, twisted shit like that. No way, she talks."

"Shit, man, rousting her ass is better than sitting around on our asses." Rick added.

I understood Rick's frustration. And right now, Rick had the only idea worth pursuing.

I sat back in the motel chair and watched the news.

The phone rang.

"I got it," Rick said. On the third ring, he answered. "Yes, sir, he is right here."

"Who is it?" I asked. Rick buried the phone into the bedspread, and in a low voice said, "It's the FBI."

I reached over. With the phone still buried in the bedspread.

"This guy sounds serious," Rick said.

"What do they want?"

He shrugged and handed me the phone.

I sat on the bed. "This is Sanzeri." "This is Special Agent Barnes with the FBI's Sacramento office. How are you this evening?"

"Fine, sir."

"I need to talk to you about something," Agent Barnes said.

"Yes sir," I said eagerly. "I'm all ears."

"You've been distributing wanted posters of Paul Candler Jr. in Alabama. Is that correct?"

"It sure is."

"Well, you need to stop," Agent Barnes said emphatically. "Now."

"Excuse me, sir. Did you say stop?" I looked at Rick, confusion all over my face. "I don't understand."

"On the bottom of the poster," Barnes continued, "there's a sentence that says Paul Candler is wanted for questioning in the Yosemite Sightseer Murders. Sanzeri, what in hell gave you that idea?"

"My investigation," I said a little defensively. I didn't like the sneer I heard in his voice.

"What investigation?" Agent Barnes asked softly.

"There's a hell of a lot that connects Candler to the murders, Agent Barnes."

"Mr. Sanzeri," Agent Barnes said calmly and patiently, as if speaking to a child, "We don't want Paul Candler Jr. for the Yosemite murder case or any other case." Then, his voice turned cold. "Get rid of the posters."

I started to feel a little bullied. "Let me ask you a question, Agent Barnes, is Candler in NCIC?"

"I don't have that information, Mr. Sanzeri." He replied curtly.

"I'm still going after Candler."

"Listen to me, Sanzeri. I'm only saying this one last time: get rid of the Candler posters."

"But, Agent Barnes," I said. "I..." But, by that time, he'd hung up.

So, the FBI was tracking us. If Candler was no big deal, why the phone call? There was no way in hell that I was going to idle the wanted posters. They're tools of the trade. I filled Rick in.

"You've gotta be kidding me!" Rick exclaimed.

"Never mind," I said. "We keep printing them. Fuck the FBI. Now, let's work on your idea to shake down Candler's girlfriend."

"Aren't you going to call Jefferson County?" Rick asked.

"No, I think I just got my answer," I said.

The call from FBI Agent Barnes may have been some kind of harsh warning, but it was also a green light for us to move on Candler. With the FBI on top of us, and us on top of Candler, I was ready to execute Rick's idea.

There's no time like the present. Tonight, we were going to pay the lovely Barbara Dobbins a little visit.

CHAPTER 18

June 6, 1999
Warrior, Alabama

"SHAKE IT UP, BABY"

AT 11:40 P.M., we arrived back in Warrior, Alabama. We were the only ones on the road. It was dark and quiet and blessedly cooler than the afternoon.

Rick and I were all set for a midnight visit to the green house. I didn't anticipate any cooperation from Barbara, squeezing her or not. As far as I knew, the pair could be in Georgia, by now.

I parked on the road, about a hundred yards away, behind some bushes that protruded over a white fence. We approached quietly on foot along the roadway.

Fifty feet or so from the house, we hid behind a large deadfall next to the gravel driveway. Every light in the house was on; all the curtains were closed tight. We watched the house for a few minutes, but there were no signs of movement.

We moved toward the front porch and the curtain moved. We stopped.

"See that?" I said, whispering.

"I did," Rick said. "Somebody's home."

If we were going to enter, it should be swift and aggressive. There was a possibility Candler was here. He certainly was brazen enough. Now, with the FBI watching us, I felt obliged to take it up a notch.

"I'm kicking the door," I said.

"You sure?" Rick said.

We rarely kick doors, maybe once a year. If we believe the bad guy is in there, it's legal. And Candler could be in there. In this circumstance, it was warranted.

"You check the backdoor, and I'll check the windows," I said.

"Meet you back up front," Rick said.

I nodded as he started along the side of the house. Although

Candler was dangerous, we couldn't underestimate Barbara. Rick came back after checking the house.

"No open windows," I said.

"Nope, it's like Fort Knox," Rick said. "Backdoor is locked."

"Front door," I suggested.

"Sounds fine."

Concealing myself, I made it to the bottom of the front porch. Rick covered me from the side.

As quietly as I could, I walked up the three wooden steps. A few creaks, but otherwise, the night was still. I turned the doorknob cautiously. It was locked.

Back at the window, I put my ear against the glass. I could hear Barbara's voice. It sounded like she was on the phone.

I backed down the stairs to the walkway. Rick was about ten feet to my right. I could barely see his face. I was ready to kick in the door and pointed to my foot. Rick gestured with a nod.

With my nine-millimeter auto in my right hand, I ran up the stairs to the porch and kicked the door just above the doorknob with all my weight.

Then . . . Wham! Like hitting a stiff trampoline, I shot backwards, landing on my back. In a flash, I leaped to my feet with my weapon drawn and ran back up the steps, taking cover by the door.

Shit! I could not believe what had just happened. Like an idiot, I'd failed to notice that the front door was metal, and so was the frame.

I started banging the door, ordering Barbara to open up. Rick hustled to the backdoor to try his size twelve's.

In a few seconds, Rick opened the front door from the inside with a half-assed smile on his face. Barbara was screaming and yelling in the background.

"Get the fuck out of my house, you motherfucker," Barbara shrieked at the top of her lungs.

"Where's your boyfriend?" Rick said. "Where's Candler?"

"I'm calling the fucking cops," Barbara said.

"Where the fuck is he, Barbara?" I asked.

"Fuck you, Sanzeri," Barbara said. "You motherfuckers have no right to be here!"

"Oh, really?" I asked. "What about jumping on my twenty-five thousand dollar bond, Barbara?"

Switching gears, Rick asked, "Was that your boyfriend on the phone?"

"Fuck you, you assholes!" She screamed. "You broke into my house!"

"Your scumbag boyfriend is a felony fugitive," I reminded her. "We thought he might be here in your cozy little love nest."

"You bastard!" Her eyes were inflamed, rimmed with red.

"Who was that on the phone, Barbara?" Rick asked, again.

Even from four feet away, I could smell alcohol all over Barbara. And, from the way her eyes darted and shifted, she looked pretty doped-up. Our problem was quickly escalating and getting out of control.

"Rick, take Ms. Congeniality to her bedroom and make her sit quietly. I'm taking a look around."

Rick, put his hand out to direct her. She responded by pushing it away.

"Touch me again, and you'll be making a dental appointment," Rick said.

My partner was a former Marine, a Vietnam Vet, and had served as Sheriff for Eureka County, Nevada. He was a family man and a good friend, with the disposition of a teddy bear (at home). In the field, my partner was no one to mess with.

"Fuck off!" Barbara said.

"No, you fuck-off and do what we tell you," Rick said. "Cooperate or go to jail for harboring a felon."

I needed to know who she was talking to, and the caller ID next to the phone gave me the answer. There were eleven calls saved, and four came from the "Days Inn" motel in Birmingham, the most recent, two minutes ago. It had to be Candler.

I went into the bedroom, where Rick and Barbara were in the middle of a quiet conversation. Surprisingly, she was crying.

Rick had that effect sometimes. He can be a real Teddy Bear.

"Paul made me run away from you guys", Barbara was saying. "He makes me do a lot of things." She sobbed.

Rick and I looked at each other.

"Why so crazy fast?" Rick asked gently. "Paul's only running on Steve's bond. So, what's the big deal?"

"A guy named Orb Hatton, that's the big deal," Barbara said. "Hatton's wanted to kill Paul for years. He used to be a Modesto cop, a narc. Paul thought you guys were down here with him."

"Come on," I said. "I don't think Orb Hatton would chase Paul all the way out here."

"Well, *you* did!" Barbara shot back.

"Fair enough," I said. "So back to the question, what in the hell are you doing in Warrior, Alabama?"

"Paul can't do any more time," Barbara said sadly.

"He's only looking at a year at most," I said. "Paul can do that standing on his head. Come clean, Barbara. I don't think you were frantically escaping us because of Orb or Paul's fear of doing time. What is it Barbara?"

She didn't answer, but clutched her flimsy robe closely to her chest.

"What's the real reason for moving to Alabama?" Rick continued gently in his best good cop voice. "It won't hurt to tell us. You're not in any trouble right now."

Barbara turned away. She picked up a pillow and began to sob into it. Then, she looked up at us, wiping her tears on the pillowcase. She sighed.

"Paul thought you guys were the feds, the FBI. He thought you were after him," Barbara said.

"For what?" I asked, feeling that tremor of excitement that had been haunting me ever since February.

"I, I can't…say…" She hesitated.

"Tell me," I said.

"No," She sobbed some more.

"Come on," I said. "Say it. The feds are chasing him, why?"

"Barbara," Rick looked at her earnestly with his sympathetic blue eyes, "You need to tell us."

"Barbara," I said as gently as I could. Barbara looked directly into my eyes and then at Rick.

"It's about that case where the three women were murdered in Yosemite." She shuddered and clutched the pillow.

An icy chill ran down my spine.

"What about the women in Yosemite?" I said, trying to suppress my excitement. She hesitated again.

"Barbara?" Rick encouraged her to continue.

60

"You know, the sightseers that were killed," Barbara choked out, her eyes red with weeping or…whatever she was taking. "The mother, the daughter, and their friend. Paul felt bad for them."

"Felt bad," I said, "what's that mean?"

"He felt sorry they got killed," Barbara said. "The pressure got to him."

"What pressure?" Rick said.

"Cops and FBI agents all over the place asking questions, talking to everyone," Barbara said. "So we left."

"He's involved, isn't he?" I asked.

She didn't answer for a moment, but I could see she suddenly realized she'd said way too much. She threw down the pillow, eyes blazing.

"You need to talk to us," Rick said. "What do you know about the murders?"

"What kind of fucking question is that? It's time for you fuckers to leave."

Her makeup was running, her tits were halfway out her nightgown, and her hair was a matted red mess.

"Get out!" she screamed. When we didn't move, she started for the door.

"Stay the fuck away from me," Barbara warned with a snarl, as she walked out.

We backed off; Barbara walked past us and into the living room. She didn't take her wild eyes off us. It was as if she'd turned into the devil. One minute, she was sobbing and sorry, the next, she was crazed with fear and anger.

We followed her into the kitchen where she lit a cigarette.

"If Paul's involved with the murders," I said gently, "you need to talk to us."

"Get the fuck out of my house. I'm not talking to you . . . Get Out!" she screeched. Then, she reached for one of the kitchen drawers. I tensed.

"Barbara, don't open that," I said. "We're leaving."

Rick and I backed out of the kitchen and left the house.

"I really didn't want to shoot her," Rick said.

"Me either," I said, as we walked to the sidewalk. I was in shock over Barbara's statements. She'd been a little whacked, but her statements were spontaneous and believable.

"What the fuck, Rick," I said. "I knew Candler was involved."

"I can't believe what we just heard." Rick shook his head.

"We need to think about heading toward Birmingham," I said. "Candler's at the Days Inn."

As I took my long awaited pinch of Copenhagen, three Jefferson County Sheriff's units arrived: Deputies Giradoux, Concord, and Deeson. Three guys who looked like brothers: all blonde, blue-eyed, built like NFL linemen. Rick and I pulled out our identifications preparing to explain our presence.

"Gentlemen," Deputy Giradoux stepped toward us.

"I'm Steve Sanzeri, and this is my partner, Rick Janes. We're conducting a bounty investigation."

"We know," Deputy Concord piped in. "Is he here?"

"Nope," Rick said, "we lost him yesterday afternoon, but his girlfriend Barbara is home. She's a little upset."

"Who called you guys?" I said.

"It just came in, 911, a home invasion," Giradoux folded his beefy arms across his chest. "We had an idea it might be you guys."

From this revelation, I knew that the warrant had been entered into NCIC. The fact that Bill Carlson didn't notify me was no real surprise. Maybe Agent Barnes and company wanted Candler for themselves.

"Any weapons in the house?" Deputy Concord asked.

"We didn't see any," Rick said. "But I'd watch out for what's in the kitchen drawer."

"We're going have a talk with her," Giradoux said. "What's her name?"

"Barbara Dobbins," Rick told him.

They turned to go into the house. I stopped them with a question.

"Just curious," I asked, "when was the warrant entered into NCIC?"

"We got the warrant handed to us at lineup," Deputy Concord put in. "I went on at seven."

Rick looked at me with a gleam of satisfaction in his eyes. We had ourselves a manhunt.

"Does Barbara have any warrants?" Deputy Deeson asked.

"Not that I know of," I said.

The deputies approached the porch. Mouth loads of obscenities bombarded them as they climbed the stairs to meet the "beast." Barbara was frothing as she came out onto the porch.

"Those fucking assholes kicked down my doors and pushed me around," Barbara shouted. "I want them arrested right now!" She spluttered and pointed at me, causing her flimsy gown to fall open.

"That one!" She paused dramatically. "That one tried to grab my tits." Seeing that she was revealing the very items she claimed I'd tried to grab, she clutched her gown and glared at me.

"Take it easy, Barbara," Giradoux said. "It's late, and you don't have to yell. Is Paul Candler your boyfriend?"

"Yeah, so!"

"Where is he?" Deeson demanded.

"Fuck you!" Barbara said.

"That's not very polite, ma'am. Now, I don't want to ask you again. Where is he?" Deeson repeated.

"Even if I knew, I wouldn't tell you anyway," Barbara said.

Barbara flipped us the bird and slammed the front door. We could still hear her cussing and yelling inside.

"Well, now, that woman is as drunk as a skunk," Deputy Concord commented, as he walked down the steps. "We could take her in, but we're not going to get shit out of her."

As we walked to the patrol cars, I noticed something familiar in Deputy Giradoux's right hand.

"Is that a wanted poster, deputy?" I asked.

The deputy unrolled the paper. "Sure is," he said, as he handed it to me.

"Un-fucking-believable," I said. "Rick, look at this."

"No way," Rick said.

"Deputy," I said. "This is what the FBI ordered me to stop printing."

"Is that right?" Deeson said. "Well, your boy is important to somebody. We all got a copy of your wanted poster. They were handed out during watch."

Seven hours earlier, the FBI told me to cease distributing the wanted posters. Now they were the playbooks for a statewide manhunt.

Before the deputies took off, I asked them to check the 911 call that brought them to Barbara's house. A minute later, Jefferson County dispatch transmitted.

"William-20 . . . county," the dispatcher said.

"William-20, go," Giradoux answered.

"William-20, the 911 caller is a, 'Dave Geer.' The call originated from the "Days Inn" in Birmingham . . . copy."

"10-4," Giradoux answered.

I informed the deputies that Dave Geer and Paul Candler were one in the same.

"How do you know this?" Deputy Deeson asked.

"The last call on the caller ID was from the "Days Inn," I said.

"I'll be dammed," Concord whistled.

The deputies wished us luck and took off with their emergency lights whirling. They were en route to Birmingham, after my bail jumper, and that felt good.

I'd just handed over a hot lead, and I had plenty of confidence the deputies would succeed. I laughed out loud as Rick and I drove away, Barbara's obscenities fading in the distance.

We couldn't get help a day ago, and now the cops were stepping on their dicks trying to catch this dirt-bag. If they caught Candler, it would be fine with me. I just needed off the bond.

Sure, I wanted Candler for many reasons, but the chance of us apprehending him now, by ourselves, was almost impossible. Furthermore, the unsolved Yosemite murders, Candler's presence in Sumiton, Alabama (the go-to "hit" capital of the US), and the strange behavior of the FBI created a puzzle that probably cut us out of the deal.

We'd take our shot at finding, "Dave Geer," anyway. It was a second chance, and a second chance is better than no chance at all.

CHAPTER 19

June 7, 1999
Birmingham, Alabama

"ENDINGS AND BEGINNINGS"

OUR SECOND CHANCE came and went without capturing Candler. By this time, I was about ready to chew through solid steel to get this guy.

We thought we'd tracked him to a Days Inn in Birmingham using Barbara's caller ID, but checking out the motel was a wash for Candler. Realizing there was another Days Inn 15 minutes away, we rallied with the local cavalry and discovered that a "Dave Geer" was registered there.

We did it by the book, but all we found was an ice-cold six-pack of beer and a bed that hadn't even been slept in. We were back to square one. Shit. I sat on the bed and helped myself to one of the brewskies.

After a lot of head-scratching, Sergeant Williams from Jefferson County and Lieutenant Pepper with his Birmingham Officers, agreed that the manhunt would continue the next day in the swamps, the snake infested swamps.

That idea did not fill me with eager pleasure. So, just before dawn, when my partner suggested that we check out the motels on Highway 131, I thought, Shit! This beats snakes.

Rick's plan had led us to the Motel-6, where sweet Maxine had finally recovered from the shock of realizing there was a murderer in her motel.

"That's him," she said, trembling and horrified that a criminal might be staying in her motel.

"Take it easy Maxine," Rick said, "you're safe."

"Oh, my Lord! I remember him!"

Maxine said. "He looked strange; he was all wet. Why, he smelt just like the dang swamp!"

"What room?" I asked. For a moment she simply stared at me as if she couldn't understand what I was saying.

"Maxine, what room?" I asked her again.

She glanced at the computer screen. "Uh, 101, room 101," Maxine said.

"Are you positive?" I said.

"I am," Maxine said. "Look, it's right here." She pulled out the registry cards.

I looked at one that was signed "Dave Geer." I turned to Rick and nodded. "Let's make the call."

While I was on the phone with Sergeant Williams, Rick asked Maxine to make another keycard for Room 101.

"We're at the Motel-6 and he's here," I said into my phone.

"Are you positive he's there?" Sergeant Williams asked.

"Affirmative," I said. "Candler checked-in under the name of Dave Geer, at 03:39 hours. The clerk recognized his photo."

"Ya'll just standby, Mr. Sanzeri. We'll be there in half an Alabama minute," Sergeant Williams told me with a strong southern drawl.

In about 30 minutes, the lobby of the Motel-6 had turned into a command post filled with at least 20 cops. Sergeant Williams, a burly bald-headed guy was running the show. Everybody else was talking and gulping coffee until Lieutenant Pepper arrived.

There was a lot of side conversation until Sergeant Williams stood up and said, "Listen up!" The room grew quiet. "Our guy is holed up in room 101. It's in the back. We got more units responding, but we need to set up a perimeter now 'cause it's getting light. We probably got about ten minutes."

Lieutenant Pepper stepped to Sergeant Williams' side. A lean man with a pencil thin mustache, he spoke with a high nasal twang. "That's right, Sergeant. We gonna need to set up a perimeter."

Sergeant Williams nodded. "Right, Bill. Most of us gotta get a position on that hill to provide fire cover if necessary. I want at least four of you at the door and four more behind. We know he's armed, and we know he's expecting us." He paused and looked around the room. "All right boys, he's cornered like a Mississippi bear. That makes him dangerous."

"Sergeant," I said. All heads swiveled to take me in: the kid from California. "My partner and I will take entry."

Rick looked at me and smiled wryly as if to say. "Thanks

partner."

"Fine," Sergeant Williams said. "Officers King and Victors. You go with Sanzeri and Janes."

I looked over at the two Officers. They looked pretty green to me.

"Gentlemen," Lieutenant Pepper said, "Paul Candler is Alabama's number one fugitive. Therefore, he's our number one concern. The feds want him for the murder of those poor women out in Yosemite National Park, California. Use any means necessary to capture him," he paused and scanned the room before adding, "including deadly force."

Sergeant Williams issued more orders, "Gallo, Redmond, and Jones. Ya'll back up the entry team—that's Sanzeri and Janes, Officers King and Victors. The rest of us will take the hill as backup. SWAT's been notified. The ETA for Birmingham SWAT is one hour. Jefferson County Tac Team, a little longer."

Shit, I thought. Anything could happen in an hour.

"O.K., everyone set?" Lieutenant Pepper asked. "Any questions?" He looked around the room, then added, "Candler's going to run or shoot at the first sight of us. All units on the hill, shut down your lights at the lower road and turndown your radios. Cover the entry team with only your rifles. No 12 gauges."

The room fell silent as the men listened.

I could feel the adrenaline simmer in my gut as Sergeant Williams continued. "The door and windows are your target areas," he said, looking flat-eyed like a water moccasin. "Sanzeri, you get the hell outta there if shots are fired, you hear?"

"Copy that," I said. I looked over at King and Victors. They were wet behind the ears with zits on their chins. Probably not even shaving yet.

Shit, I thought, the last thing I wanted was rookies at entry, the most dangerous position. But it wasn't my call. Hell, I'd asked for it. At least it was Rick and me at point. This wasn't his first rodeo; we'd been in this position before.

It was 5:30 a.m. and getting lighter. We had our assignments. It looked like I would be getting another chance at my fugitive. Suddenly, I had one of those weird feelings that it was going to get messy.

"Let's hustle up," I said. It was almost sunrise as I led Rick and the officers up the long steep driveway. I picked up the pace as we approached the last building. Sliding along the wall, I peeked around the corner. In the distance, I could hear the muffled sounds of patrol cars arriving on the hill. I slipped under a window to the left of the door to room 101.

Rick covered the right side. Officers Victors and King took separate positions behind the brush about 20 feet behind. Everyone was in place. We had our marching orders to stay-put and wait for SWAT, but I wasn't so sure that was going to happen. Time was not on our side.

I thought about Candler, who was probably sweating it out right now inside. He'd done time, and he was in good physical shape. It might not be all that easy running him down.

Tactical entry was the plan if Candler couldn't be talked out, which I was sure wasn't his plan. And if Candler busted out of the room, it was on us. As more and more units arrived on the hill, I didn't feel any safer. I have been in this same position a few times and the anticipation and waiting is what gets on your nerves. But it was never quite like this, not with the amount of firepower pointed at my back.

Officer Victors received radio traffic and then signaled to me that the hill was ready. I looked up. The sun was starting to show itself above the tree line over the hill. I could barely make out the patrol cars.

I watched the doorknob and the curtains, alert for the slightest signs of movement. I looked at my watch and only five minutes had passed, but it felt more like a half-hour. My gun-hand was sweaty. Units were still arriving, and I was hoping that Candler didn't hear the crunching of gravel from the hill. I wanted this thing over with soon.

I signaled to Rick, and he handed me the key. The number written on the card was 301. Wrong fucking key. Maxine must have been so confused, she'd coded in the wrong room. Great!

Without saying a word, I tossed it back to Rick, and he took off for the office.

Officers Victors and King had good concealment and that was a good thing, but I was surprised that neither stepped up to fill Rick's position. Fucking rookies.

I noticed the curtain move. With my finger pointed toward the window, I signaled to the officers who tensed, sweat pouring off their young faces. The curtain moved again, and I aimed at the window.

Then, the door lock clicked and the doorknob turned slowly. I took a step back against the wall with my weapon pointed at the door. Gripping my 9 mm auto tighter, I took a slow breath.

Suddenly the door flew open, and Candler leaped out! He went straight at me, reaching for my gun. I turned away and I grabbed his throat with my left hand, keeping my weapon away from his grasp.

We went down. I grabbed the back of his head as we fell, smashing his face into the gravel.

I've never fought a wild cat, but this was what it must be like. Candler cursed, spat, and tried to bite me. He tried to roll me over as we fought. Man, it was hard to keep him down while holding my gun away from his eager hands.

Then, it felt like my old football team had arrived. A tremendous pounding of large bodies piled on top of us. It was the corn-fed Alabama Calvary, the cops. I peeled myself out from under the dog-pile as officers and deputies tried to restrain Candler, but he didn't give up; he just kept on fighting.

I secured my weapon, caught my breath, and jumped back in. I saw an opening and dropped my right knee onto the back of Candler's neck. He went limp. I grabbed his left wrist and cuffed it. A deputy hooked the other wrist, looked up at me, and winked.

Turning to Candler's red face, the deputy drawled, "Don't fight us, boy, it's over with."

These were words I wanted to hear. The most dangerous bounty hunt I'd ever encountered was over indeed, but the rest of the story had only just begun.

CHAPTER 20

June 7, 1999
Birmingham, Alabama

"A CONFESSION?"

I FELT A lot of satisfaction after we'd nabbed Candler; I was especially glad that he hadn't gotten my gun and shot me when he burst through the door.

Rick's idea to visit hotel row was genius. Paul Candler Jr. was finally in custody. I never had such a struggle in my life or for my life. No one had ever tried to take my weapon and I never had to physically takedown a fugitive who was running on a murder beef.

I shook Rick's hand. "Great job partner," I said.

"Same to you," Rick said.

We both turned and watched as Candler was directed against the wall and searched by deputies. We joined Lieutenant Pepper and Sergeant Williams.

Sergeant Williams spoke to Rick. "Man, that asshole came at your partner like a Tasmanian Devil."

I walked over to Paul Candler, who was handcuffed and sitting on the ground leaning against the building. He was bleeding from the mouth, nose and middle of his forehead.

"God damn, Paul," I said, "you look like shit. Running is hard business, ain't it?"

"Fuck you, motherfucker," Candler said. "Take these fucking cuffs off, and let's go again. Come on!"

"I'll tell you what fuckhead," I said, "maybe next time I'll just shoot you."

Candler tried to stand up, but one of the deputies pushed him down hard.

"Fuck all you mother fuckers," Candler snarled. "I'll kill all of you!" He turned to Rick and me. "You two are dead! Hear me? Fucking dead."

"O.K., cool it," Sergeant Williams said.

"Hey, fuck you too," Candler said.

70

"You want to fuck me?" Sergeant Williams said. "What are you, some kind of California surfer faggot? You came here to get fucked in the ass? Well boy, you just got fucked in the ass. Get this piece of shit out of my sight."

Lieutenant Pepper turned to Sergeant Williams and asked who would be transporting Candler to the hospital. Candler was my responsibility, so I offered my services. They were relieved.

As expected, it was no joyride to the hospital. I drove with Candler in the passenger seat, cuffed and shackled. Rick sat behind him, within arms' reach of a chokehold.

Candler never shut up. He told us that he was going to kick our asses, kill us, fuck our mothers, kill our kids. Blah, blah, blah. I wanted to shove his head through the windshield.

It was 6:20 a.m. when we entered the waiting room at Birmingham General Hospital. The hospital was in a tough neighborhood, and the security guards were armed. It was busy for such an early morning; there were two stabbing victims in front of us.

"Take a seat, Candler," I said, "it'll be a while."

"I could give a fuck," Candler said. "Get me something to eat."

"If you calm down," Rick said.

"I will," Candler said. "Get me some candy bars, and I'll fucking calm down."

None of us had eaten for hours, and I left in search of the vending machines. When I returned with pockets full of snacks, Rick was standing outside of the waiting room. He had a shit-eating grin on his face.

"Here, let me help you," Rick said.

"I got it," I said. "What's up?"

"Let's feed Paul, and I'll tell you."

Candler was cooperating, so Rick moved the handcuffs to the front.

"What kind of candy bar do you want?" Rick said.

"Anything," Candler said, "and give me one of those fucking sodas."

Rick gave me the wink. "Excuse us for a minute," he told Candler.

We left the room, and I closed the glass door behind us.

"What's going on?" I asked curiously.

"Paul and I had a little discussion, and you're going to like what he told me."

"OK!" I said.

"While you were dropping quarters in the machine," Rick said, "I took a shot and asked Paul why he ran to Alabama. He first told me to fuck my mother a bunch of times and to kiss his hairy ass."

"What else is new?" I said.

"I kept after him, and I could see he wanted to say something, so I kept prying."

"Tell me man, what did he say?"

"He said he thought we were Feds and wanted to question him about the Yosemite murders," Rick paused for effect. "Then, he said that he felt sorry for them."

"Them?" I asked, feeling a twist in my guts.

"The girls," Rick answered.

"You have got to be kidding," I said. "He said that? Fuck, man, those are the same statements as Barbara's. The motherfucker's involved. I knew it. Damn Rick! What did we get ourselves into?"

"I thought I was hearing things," Rick said, "but that's exactly what he said."

"Candler's involved," I said, "no doubt about that now." I thought about the phone call from Agent Barnes the night before. He'd tried to call us off, but was following our every move.

"It all adds up. The FBI wants Candler, and they use local law enforcement and us to find him."

Within an hour and a half, Candler was treated and released back into our custody, with three stitches above his right eye. Fifteen minutes later, we arrived at the Fultondale Police Department.

"You sure are quiet, Paul," Rick said. "Don't you want to talk about it anymore?"

"I have nothing to say to you assholes."

"Tell Steve, what you told me," Rick said.

"Sorry, I forgot what I said," Candler said. "Oh, I remember, go fuck yourselves."

I didn't need to hear any more from Candler; I was satisfied and had no plans to fuck around with him any longer than necessary. Soon, he wouldn't be my problem.

72

Candler's statement was a carbon copy of what Barbara had told us earlier. That was good enough for me. I watched as Rick directed our prisoner through the jail entrance.

At last, I thought, the Feds and law enforcement will put two-and-two together and figure out who the suspects are. I knew Candler was dirty, and I thought it was only a matter of time until all the dirt-bags who were involved would be rounded up to face justice. I couldn't have been more wrong.

CHAPTER 21

June 7, 1999
Sumiton, Alabama

"HOT STORY"

ONCE BACK AT our hotel room, I opened some beers and we had a small celebration along with some pizza. Again, I praised Rick for his motel idea. Sleep was next on the list, but, as I went to close the curtains, I noticed a satellite truck enter the parking lot. I saw two more vans approaching from the highway.

"Hey Rick," I said, "check this out."

Rick stood behind me.

"Holy cow," Rick said, "for us?

"I would guess. Don't let them see you." Within five minutes there were four television new satellite units in the parking lot of our motel.

"How the hell did they find us?" I said.

"The FBI knows," Rick said. "That must mean everybody knows."

I watched as the news crews entered the motel lobby. Then, the phone rang.

"This is Bruce, at the front desk. There are some people from the TV stations that want to talk to you."

"Can you get rid of them?" I asked.

"Sure. I'll try," Bruce said.

"Good," I said, "tell them we checked-out."

"Not a problem, I'll take care of it."

Rick and I had already discussed this exact situation if we caught Candler. Ignoring the press was a must. I didn't want to be responsible for aiding and abetting hungry journalists in pursuit of giving the FBI a black eye. A couple of bounty hunters capturing a murderer before the FBI grabbed him would cause a stir.

After catching some "Z's", we watched the ten and eleven o'clock news. Candler's arrest was top story, but the FBI downplayed him as a suspect in the Yosemite murders.

FBI Special Agent Nick Rossi, stated, "Paul Candler Jr. is not a suspect in the Yosemite Sightseer Case. The FBI was not seeking his arrest from any warrants generated by the taskforce. Paul Candler is only wanted for questioning with regards to information about the case."

Even though we both knew Candler was involved somehow, we flew back to California the next morning not suspecting that another link in the Yosemite Sightseer's Murder investigation would show itself soon.

I had several phone messages from newsgroups my first morning back and they continued for about five days. I didn't owe the press any explanations, but I was getting tired of avoiding them.

I was convinced that Candler was involved with the Yosemite Case, and I wanted to expose him, so I decided to do one press release via AP (Associated Press). "Bay Area News" of San Francisco, ran with my story and put it over the wire. I was satisfied that they had the entire story of how we captured Paul Candler. It was all I was saying for now.

By the end of June, investigators had reviewed the testimonies and evidence linked to several of the suspects' in-custody. The FBI's Special Agent in Charge, James Maddock, stated during a press release, *While no one has yet been charged, we feel that those responsible for the killings of Carole Sund, Juli Sund and Silvina Pelosso, are already behind bars.*

That was fine with me. I knew Candler was behind bars, along with eight other suspects. What I didn't understand was that nobody was being charged with the murders.

Investigators continued to shakeup the central valley's methamphetamine trade with hopes of getting more to work with, but their efforts continued to be futile. Then, three weeks after Maddock's statement, there was a turn in the case. This twisted the Yosemite investigation like nothing could.

On July 22, 1999, park rangers found the decapitated body of, Joie Ruth Armstrong close to her cabin in the Yosemite community of "Foresta." Mostly populated by park workers, there had never been a serious crime committed in the area. Ever.

Twenty-six-year-old, Joie Armstrong, worked for the Yosemite Institute as a Naturalist. Investigators believe she was murdered on the evening of Wednesday July 21, and this time they had strong physical evidence.

In light of their earlier statement that all of the scumbags were jailed and accounted for, the FBI remained relatively quiet, but conceded that the case needed to be re-evaluated. James Maddock questioned whether his agency could have done anything to prevent Joie Armstrong's murder. *"I've struggled with that issue for the last 24 hours and continue to do so. I'm confident we've done everything that could be reasonably done."*

I didn't think so! What about Paul Candler? The Feds did nothing with him. Mick Larwick shot a cop, and his dumb ass half-brother, Rufus Dykes, confessed to the murders! They weren't even indicted. And now another murder in the park?

At first, I was thinking copycat crime. And then I thought The FBI has the right guys. They just missed one. Who was it?

The FBI and investigators went into overdrive and on Saturday July 24, James Maddock announced that a man was in custody that they strongly suspected was the killer of Joie Armstrong.

Cary Anthony Stayner, 37, a handyman employed by the Cedar Lodge, had been one of the people questioned in February, after Carole, Juli and Silvina went missing. At that time the FBI had no reason to suspect Cary Stayner, but after Joie Armstrong's murder, he was brought in again for questioning.

As an interesting note, Stayner's little brother, Steven Stayner, was the subject of national attention when he showed up at the Ukiah Police Station in 1983, after being held prisoner for almost seven years by a child molester named Kenneth Parnell.

Cary Stayner was only eighteen when Steven came home, bringing an incredible amount of attention with him. Cary's little brother was even the subject of a television movie, *I know My First Name is Steven*.

Psychologists began to speculate about Stayner, saying that he was actually vying for public notice by confessing to the murders, even as far back as July 1999.

"Overshadowed All His Life: Low-key Cary Stayner took back seat to Kidnapped Brother," was the title of a *San Francisco Chronicle* article.

In a review of the Ted Rowlands interview, the *Chronicle* said that Stayner "strangled two women and burned their bodies, butchered two others and wanted a TV 'movie of the week' made of his life and crimes."

It looked like Stayner was getting the attention he craved. In another bizarre twist, police reopened a 1990 case concerning Stayner's uncle, Jesse "Jerry" Stayner. Cary Stayner had been living with his uncle at the time Jesse was discovered dead in his home, slain by a shotgun blast.

Attention or not, as far as I was concerned, nothing really supported the idea that Stayner had acted alone. In fact, it was hard to believe it.

Sure Stayner was a psycho creep, but he may have confessed to stuff he didn't do.

In McDougal's book, *The Yosemite Murders*, the author comments that "at least part of his (Stayner's) matter of fact recitation of that horrifying homicidal night would quickly be exposed as a flat-out lie: that he had neither raped nor molested his victims in any way."

Stayner was involved, but what if he wasn't the one doing the molesting and the raping?

Mariposa County detectives found Cary sunbathing on the banks of the Merced River, and detained him for questioning. Looking for evidence, detectives searched his International Scout and confiscated a backpack.

Although it didn't strike the detectives at the time, the well-read novel in the backpack got a lot of attention later. It was called *Black Lightning* by John Saul, and it was about the sibling rivalry between the two murdering brothers, Rory and Richard Kraven.

The book was grisly, but it was really focused on hunting for headlines as well as hunting for heads.

I had to ask myself: What better fall guy than Cary Stayner to take the hit for other bad guys? What better stooge than a creep who wanted to make headlines for himself?

Stayner was released and told not to leave El Portal. Cary Stayner ignored the order and took off that evening.

The following day, FBI agents searched his apartment (which was located above the Cedar Lodge restaurant), and discovered evidence that linked Stayner to Armstrong's murder.

On July 24, the FBI caught up with Stayner at the "Laguna Del Sol" nudist colony in Winton, near Sacramento. The manager recognized Cary Stayner from a newscast and notified authorities. Stayner was now in custody for the murder of Joie Armstrong.

En route to FBI headquarters, Cary Stayner made incriminating statements to FBI Agent Jeff Rinek. Stayner stated that he could not resist the urge to kill Joie after he met her. In the FBI's mind, this time they had the right man. Stayner had given the FBI details only the killer would know.

Then, Stayner opened up even more and confessed to the murders of Carole Sund, Juli Sund and Silvina Pelosso. I was blown away. The FBI had all these other guys locked-up and now they were looking at only one person?

Come on. I wasn't buying it. It took more than one dirt-bag to kidnap and murder the three women. How could he kill Carole Sund and Silvina Pelosso, carry them out to the trunk of the rental car, and do it all while Juli stayed quietly in the bedroom of that single room suite?

He had to have help. Shit. He knew Mick Larwick. In fact, he knew Larwick's father, Leroy Larwick, who had lived in Long Barn, where Mick grew up. The same place where the burned up rental car was found containing the bodies of Carole Sund and Silvina Pelosso.

Stayner was pals with Dykes and Larwick. He was also fascinated by the legend of Big Foot. And, in another strange twist, Leroy Larwick, Mick's father, was a Bigfoot buff, a guy who supposedly got photos of the strange creature and his 15 minutes of fame for accomplishing it.

Rumors had it that Stayner was connected to a group of Bigfoot fanatics called the "Modesto Cranksters." And guess who the big time members were? You got it: Eugene Dykes and Mick Larwick, half-brothers, guys who hung out in Long Barn and the Cedar Lodge in El Portal.

And, since I'm putting two and two together and getting four, the Cedar Lodge was one of the few bars up in El Portal near

Yosemite. Joie Armstrong hung out there with her friends for party times. What do you think the chances are that Stayner saw her?

A lot of people, including myself, were well aware that Dykes and Larwick knew Stayner. Hell, as far I knew, Stayner and Candler could have been pals, too. Turns out, as I found out later, I wasn't that far off.

Meanwhile, along with everybody else, I followed the media frenzy surrounding Cary Stayner's arrest and confession. On November 30, 1999, he pled guilty to the federal charge of murder in the death of Joie Ruth Armstrong. In exchange for the guilty plea, prosecutors did not seek the death penalty.

The FBI wasn't saying much about the earlier suspects they named, especially the two half-brothers, Eugene "Rufus" Dykes and Michael "Mick" Larwick. Investigators had been hot and heavy over these bad boys, and I knew they were on the right track. But after Stayner's arrest, Dykes and Larwick were no longer considered suspects, nor were any of the others rounded up by the taskforce.

On July 25, 1999, a Federal Magistrate found there was enough evidence to charge Cary Stayner for the murder of Joie Armstrong. Stayner's vehicle left tire tracks that led from Joie's cabin to her deceased body. There was a lot of physical evidence against Stayner and along with his confession, the FBI had him nailed. Investigators believed that Joie's murder was committed by a single killer, and I think they were right about that.

Unfortunately, with regard to Carole, Juli and Silvina, investigators were no longer interested in any other suspects. I held out hope that the Mariposa and Tuolumne County D.A.'s would do their jobs and send Candler up the river with a few others, but it didn't look as though that was going to happen.

I was disappointed. We had compelling statements and exculpatory evidence proving Candler was involved. But the authorities wanted to look good to the public. They had their man and a confession.

For them, it was "case closed." But, for me, the case was still wide open.

Location of *Joie Armstrong's* Body

Yosemite National Park

4

120

Mt. Reba Ski Resort

207

Yosemite Valley

Bear Valley

Dorrington Long Barn

120

Twain Harte

Arnold

Murphys Buck Meadows

140

Foresta

4 108

Joie Armstrong

El Portal

Angels Camp

Groveland

Cedar Lodge

Sonora

Stayner's Residence

Melones Jamestown

49 120

Chinese Camp

Briceburg

Lake Don Pedro

108

Moccasin

49

Coulterville 140

Mariposa Airport

Murder Victim's Location

Map is not to Scale

Mt. Bullion **Mariposa**

Drawn by Stephen M. Sanzeri

49

80

CHAPTER 22

February 21, 2000
Mariposa County, California

"HE'S BACK!"

IT HAD BEEN just over a year since Carole, Juli and Silvina were murdered. I kept a close eye on the Yosemite case and remained dumbfounded. I was convinced that Stayner did not act alone, and I was sure that Candler was involved as an accomplice along with Michael Larwick, Eugene Dykes and a few others.

I needed some new leads to keep my investigation going, but I was plum out. I re-read archived news stories on the chance I might have missed something. And every so often I found something new, something I'd missed earlier, a clue that became a lead when the old information was crossed with the new.

In late February of 2000, I began contacting a few of my informants. I asked my old snitches to find me some new ones. Since the FBI and investigators had backed off, the underground had started to surface.

Soon I had a new idea. I couldn't do a thing about Candler, so why not look into the dirt-bags that the FBI had rounded-up and, then, dismissed. I targeted the half-brothers, Dykes and Larwick, and any others that landed in my lap. I planned to retrace investigators' steps and see what I could dig up.

Of course, I wouldn't be announcing what I was up to. I would wait until I gathered additional facts and evidence before I sent off anymore unanswered reports. I would be a lone wolf all the way.

Even after a year, all of the suspects the FBI believed were involved with the homicides remained in county jails or in prison for probation and parole violations, except for one.

Yeah, guess who?

It was the first week of March, and I was outside watering and sipping on Scotch when the call came in. I recognized the area code, Alabama. It was the neighbor that had lived across the road from Candler and his girlfriend, Barbara Dobbins, when they'd lived in Warrior. Man, he was pissed. He knew Candler was bad news, and he wasn't thrilled about having him back as a neighbor.

Shit, Candler was looking at prison time, at least a year for the firearm charge. What in the hell was he doing out of jail and back in Alabama?

Monday morning came early for me. As soon as I knew their office was open, I got on the phone to Bill Carlson in the Tuolumne County District Attorney's Office.

"He's a free man," Bill Carlson said in answer to my questions. "The DA decided to lower the charges, so Candler did thirty days with us."

"No state time?" I asked in disbelief. "That's it?"

"Thirty days. That was it."

I couldn't talk for a second. Finally I said, "One more question, Bill."

"Go ahead."

"Is Candler clear of all warrants?" I asked.

"Sure is, I ran him myself a month ago."

"But…" I began.

"Sorry, Sanzeri. Gotta go." Carlson hung up before I could say another word.

I thought back to the time I'd called him at the country club, back when I was tracking Candler. He ran me around the block about the NCIC. That was strange then, and I hadn't trusted him or Tuolumne County investigators ever since.

Just after nailing Candler, I caught word of a fifty-thousand dollar bench warrant out of Merced County, California for threatening to kill his mother. I made a call to an old acquaintance: Captain Petro of the Atwater Police Department – Atwater, Paul Candler's home town.

"Hey, Sanzeri. How the hell are ya?" Captain Petro asked. "Good job catching Candler!"

"You read the papers?" I said.

"Sure. We wanted him at the same time you were in Alabama. We had a felony warrant packaged and ready before Christmas. Nice one, fifty grand."

"So, what happened," I said.

"It vanished," Captain Petro said.

"Vanished?" I asked.

"Man, I don't know what happened. The case is active but the warrant was dropped. He was released without bail on our charges. It was above my pay grade. I couldn't do a thing."

Unbelievable.

CHAPTER 23

March 12, 2000
Arnold, California

"BRAZEN"

IT WAS COLD, dark, and beginning to snow, when my partner pulled into the Arnold "Shell" gas station near his home around 9:00 p.m.

Rick filled the tank and got in. As he started the car, a man flew out of the darkness and punched out the windshield with a large object and then hit the driver's door window, exploding that into flying chunks of glass.

The attacker struck Rick in the face several times, breaking his glasses and cutting him up. Rick fended him off the best he could from inside the car, finally getting it started, and driving the hell out of there.

Rick never got a good look at the asshole because it was so dark. He managed to make it home OK and his wife dressed a couple of small lacerations on his face.

He didn't go find a doc – he was too pissed off. Instead, he looked for another set of specs and his Smith & Wesson .45 caliber auto.

That was when I got the phone call. "Steve, get up here quick," Kathy said. "Rick was just attacked."

"What?" I said.

"Some guy busted out his windows at the Shell station. He's O.K., but he's cut up a little."

"No shit," I said. "Did you call the cops?"

"No! But he's really pissed. He grabbed his gun. He's looking for the punk."

"Good," I said, "don't call Calaveras; I'm on my way up."

Who the fuck did this? While en route to Arnold, I thought up a short list of dirt-bags that hated us and were brazen enough to pull such a stunt. Rick and I had a few enemies out there; it's the nature of the business.

There was no reason to bring in the Calaveras County Sheriff's Department until we took a look around for ourselves. I had a pretty good idea who jumped Rick, and Rick had to be thinking the same thing.

Yeah. About 5'10" with a lot of tattoos. A guy with a hot temper and a mean meth habit. A guy who really resented being captured in a pokey little town down Alabama way. And those threats he made; it had to be Paul Candler.

When I got to the top of Highway 4, I contacted Rick via the radio. I told him I'd meet him at the Shell station, where Marla was the clerk on duty.

I met Rick outside and checked out his face. Under the cold light of the security lamps, I could see where Kathy had slapped some small band aids over the cuts, but these didn't cover the bruises that were already forming around his eyes and forehead.

We went inside.

"I saw him attack your car," Marla said when we asked her about it. "Are you OK Rick?"

"Yeah. Thanks, I'm O.K."

"Marla, did you recognize the guy?" I asked.

"His name is Paul," Marla said.

Rick and I looked at each other.

"Paul who?" Rick asked.

"I think his last name is Chandler. He lives across the street around the corner," Marla said. "I see him in here almost every day buying beer and cigarettes." She gestured out the window. "I think he lives in the brown shake house on the corner on Manuel Mill Road."

"You said Chandler, Marla." Rick asked. "Could you mean Candler?"

"That's it!" Marla said. "Candler. Paul Candler. God, he's a real jerk; he doesn't say much – just orders his shit like some sort of rock star."

"Another thing, Marla," I said, "tell me about his tattoos."

"Oh yeah," she said. "He's got'em on both arms. One's this sort of devil tattoo and there's a spider web on his elbow. Kinda creepy."

It was Candler, one-hundred percent.

Rick and I watched the Manuel Mill house across Highway 4 and the Shell station until late morning. All quiet. The house looked vacant. There were some junkie old cars and a green ford pickup in the front yard, and that was it. Nothing stirring, so we packed it in for the night.

The next day after Rick cooled down, he decided to report the incident and met with a Calaveras County Sheriff's Deputy.

Rick may have cooled off, but the chicken-shit attack on my partner fueled anger in me like a torch to a gas tank. Something like this had never happened before, and, frankly, it scared me. Sure, bail jumpers had threatened us in the past. Most are all talk, but not Paul Candler.

I couldn't stop thinking: If Candler had been carrying a gun, Rick might be dead.

"So what happened?" I asked, when Rick phoned after the deputy had left.

"I don't think the deputy believed me," Rick said.

"About what?" I said.

"About the bounty. He had a hard time swallowing the fact that Candler would threaten us and then follow through with an attack. The damn deputy almost starting laughing."

"What a dick," I said. "It usually doesn't happen, but this time it did. This time, it was an attack based on opportunity – one of the worst kinds, Rick."

I stared out my living room window, but I didn't see the Manzanita-covered hillsides. I could only picture the image of Candler attacking my partner. I went on. "He saw you, he recognized you, and he decided to redecorate your car and your face at the same time. What about Marla? What about what she saw?"

"I told the deputy about her," Rick said, "but, it was kind of weird."

"What was weird?" I said.

"It was like the deputy knew Candler. I told him how Marla witnessed the attack. But, when I mentioned Candler, he hesitated. Then, he said that, according to the witness, the guy's name was "Chandler.""

Rick laughed bitterly and went on. "Then, the deputy said that Marla was a 'lowlife' and an unreliable witness."

"Mother fucker!" I exclaimed.

"No, shit," Rick said. "I told that deputy everything that happened. I showed him my busted up car and my busted up face! Then, he just straight up, said that I was wrong. Fucker pissed me off."

Calaveras County is a small place, maybe forty-thousand residents. The cops know all the scumbags. They knew Paul Candler.

"Calaveras County is fucking protecting Candler." I said.

"You got it," Rick said.

After four days, the Calaveras County Deputy informed Rick that there would be no charges filed on Paul Candler or Paul Chandler, or anyone else for that matter.

Marla had retracted her statement saying she didn't recognize Rick's assailant. She was probably scared shitless. I was disappointed, but I understood.

It was now obvious that the Sheriff's Office had covered-up the attack on my partner for political reasons surrounding the closed Yosemite Sightseer Investigation. The last thing the FBI wanted was another can of worms opened up. With no charges filed against Paul Candler, there would be no story about the arresting bounty hunter that was attacked 2,400 miles away from Alabama.

A story like this would make great copy for the papers. But, the FBI directed Calaveras County to squash the allegations against Paul Candler.

Lack of constitutional responsibility by the Calaveras County Sheriff's Department and the FBI had placed Rick and me in more danger than ever. My number one priority was to stay alive.

For the first time in a long time, a firearm never left my side. Along with my 12 gauge shotgun in the corner of my office, I had a .45 in my top desk drawer. The most dangerous man I'd ever chased was living eight miles up the road and the cops were protecting him.

Then, on June 3, 2000, a jury found Paul Candler Jr. guilty of the continuous sexual molestation of a 12-year-old girl. This was a case out of Merced County. Candler was sentenced to 17-years in the Tehachapi State Prison in California and became a lifelong member of the 290 PC (sex registrant) club.

Turns out, when they locked-up Candler, a bunch of aliases where discovered. These names included: Paul Leckey Candler, Paul Candles, Paul Chandler, Paul L. Chandler, Paul Leckey Chandler, Paul Lackey Chandler and Paul Leckley Chandler.

Well I couldn't complain too much at this point. At least the motherfucker had gotten nailed. He was a convicted pedophile and rapist, and, for me, this certainly added credence to his involvement in the Yosemite murders. Now, with Candler out of the way, Rick and I could relax a little.

I was ready to jump back into the investigation.

CHAPTER 24

July 9, 2000
Stanislaus County, California

"A HIRED KILLER?"

RICK AND I went to the central valley, stopping in the cow towns, searching for connections, and visiting as many depressing trailer parks as we could handle. We focused on well-known dope areas like Keyes, Salida, Empire, and Turlock.

We tried to develop new contacts, but it wasn't working. We marked a lot of serious hours, but we just couldn't get close to anyone.

Then on July 9, 2000, my faith in the snitch network jumped several notches. One of my people delivered me a gift named "Phil."

The call came from Mark, an old bail client of mine, who still had connections in the valley dope trade. I'd called him to snoop around for me, and he did. He owed me one from a bond I posted last year.

"This ain't no long shot, Steve," Mark said as he whispered into the phone. "Take a look at the doctor that was found dead at Bear Valley last year. You remember?"

"I remember," I said, "Doctor Wong was her name, and this has to do with what?"

"I read the papers, don't you?" Mark asked.

"All the time." I said. I could picture him at a pay phone, looking around nervously.

"Find the June 9, *Sonora Ledger*," Mark said.

"O.K. But, what's your point?"

Mark waited a few seconds. "Look, man, check out the discovery of Wong's body."

I remembered reading the story of Wong's disappearance when Rick and I were in Modesto on a bounty. How could I forget? It was in my own backyard. I also remembered that there'd been hardly any press.

That was strange, because Dr. Wong disappeared on February 19, the same day Carole Sund's billfold was discovered. The Sund and Pelosso party had disappeared on February 15, only four days earlier.

The distance between Yosemite Village and Mt. Reba is about a three hour drive. The distance from Arnold to Mt. Reba is about forty-five minutes. Modesto is two hours from Mr. Reba.

And what connection is this?" I prompted him, already getting the picture.

"I know the deputy who found the doctor's body." He paused. "Dude, this deputy said the doctor was murdered, man."

I'd saved the June 9, *Sonora Ledger Dispatch* because it was right around the time we caught Candler.

"Dr. Wong was murdered?" I repeated.

"Yeah, man," Mark whispered. "Word is it's your boy, the one you nailed down in Alabama." He paused, concluding. "O.K., man, that's one less I owe you. We're even man. Phil will call you."

Mark disconnected before I could respond.

I stood there, the phone glued to my ear, chills running down my spine. Doctor Katherine Wong's body was discovered on June 8, 1999, one day after we nailed Candler in Fultondale, Alabama, the acknowledged hit-for-hire capital of the United States. There it fucking was.

Finally, I took the cell phone from my hand, folded it, and put it back in my pocket. Then, I just stood there, looking out at the hills, and thinking.

Law enforcement and district attorneys make deals all the time. It's the way they do business: You cooperate with us; we'll cooperate with you.

I recalled my March 1999 phone call with Bill Carlson, where he'd revealed that all warrants on Candler had vanished. I remembered my call to Captain Petro in Atwater, when he described the nicely packaged felony warrant that had dematerialized.

Everybody'd been interested in Candler at one time. Then, poof!

I thought about the strange June 1999 phone call from the FBI Special Agent Barnes when Rick and I were in Alabama. Barnes had asked me to stop distributing wanted posters that included the phrase: "wanted for questioning in the Yosemite Murders." He'd said that the FBI did not want Candler for questioning in any case. I

90

knew that Candler had given the FBI Dr. Wong's body. The timing of his capture and subsequent release was too smooth.

Candler had lived in the town of Arnold, and Arnold is only 45 minutes from Mt. Reba (Bear Valley). In remote and sparsely populated areas, that distance is nothing.

It was very odd that no one in the media had made any mention that Wong's disappearance and the disappearances of Carole, Juli and Silvina were only four days apart.

Three women disappear from a tourist lodge in Yosemite. Four days later, another woman disappears from a ski resort just a couple of hours away. Both places are tourist destinations; both places are located in similar remote areas.

But the most telling coincidence of all was that, on June 8, 1999, the day after Candler was arrested in Alabama, an unidentified person found Wong's body in Bear Valley.

What else did Candler give them? What did they trade for what? Looking back over time, I saw that Paul Candler had been handled in a suspiciously different way. Why had he been protected from involvement in these investigations?

Candler was involved in the Yosemite Murders or knew a lot about them. And he either murdered Doctor Wong, or he knew who did.

They say there's no such thing as coincidence. That may or may not be true. But, when the coincidences start piling up in multiple numbers, they create a picture that's hard to ignore.

Either way, I felt bound to follow up.

CHAPTER 25

July 13, 2000
Angels Camp, California

"WHAT REALLY HAPPENED TO DR. WONG?"

AFTER TALKING WITH Mark, "Phil," the ex-Alpine County Deputy involved with the Doctor Wong investigation, called.

Phil agreed to meet me at an overlook on Highway 49, above New Melones Reservoir, about four miles outside of Angels Camp. I pulled in at 5:00 p.m. that evening, and saw him leaning against his Cherokee. I parked and walked over to shake hands with him.

Phil was a tall, nice-looking guy, with sandy hair and a face that had seen a lot of sun.

He straightened up when he saw me and leaned over to shake hands. He didn't smile, and he seemed tense, lines of worry etched around his bright green eyes.

After a brief moment, I started in.

"You look like this Wong case has you bugged," I said.

"I am bugged," Phil said, pinching the bridge of his nose. "I've been hiding since I learned that the insurance company wants to talk to me."

"Why?" I asked.

"There are several reasons and the sheriff is the first."

"The sheriff?" I asked, "The Alpine County Sheriff?"

"Yup," he sighed and squinted as he looked over at the lake. "I guess I should start at the beginning." He looked uncomfortable, and he scuffed the dirt with his boot.

"Phil, how about a beer?" I asked, trying to put him at ease.

"That would be great."

I opened the hatch to my Nissan Pathfinder and slid out the ice chest.

"Have a cold one," I said.

"Thanks," Phil said.

Phil took a long pull and cleared his throat. Then, he took another sip. After that, he dove right in.

"It wasn't until four o'clock in the afternoon that the husband reported his wife missing. Neither he, nor their kids had seen mom for several hours. Apparently, they were all pretty decent skiers."

"Yeah," I commented. "But, even good skiers get lost sometimes."

"True," he said. "Skiers ignore the signs and ski out of bounds. Every weekend someone gets lost up there, but we find them within hours. And, that's a record I'm proud of."

"She and her husband were on the same run at the same time, so he says. They were going to meet at the bottom, but she never showed up."

He took another pull on the beer and wiped his thin mouth with the back of his hand. "Our search and rescue team worked throughout the night and for five days after that. We never found her."

"Was she like one of those off-the-trail renegade skiers?" I asked.

"Nah, not really," Phil said. "She was too smart. From my experience, it's the fucking idiots and drunks who get loaded on weed and wine that need to be rescued. Not someone like her."

"When did you start to suspect foul play?" I said.

"Not the first day, not really, but after a week, I started to think she might not even be there. I was the only person in the Sheriff's Department thinking that this was a kidnapping or possible homicide."

"What prompted your thoughts?" I said.

"Shit, man. The disappearances of the three women were just four days earlier. It ain't that far from Yosemite to Bear Valley."

I nodded my head in agreement. Those were my exact thoughts.

"I interviewed the husband," Phil continued, "and that was fishy to start with. He didn't seem worried at all, and he was real short with his answers. I know everybody handles the disappearance of a loved one or a spouse differently, but this guy was cold."

"Was it stormy, snowing hard that day?" I said.

"That's another thing," he was animated now. "It was a clear day with blue skies. It was warm, a great day for skiing. There was no wind. Let me tell you Steve, No one gets lost on days like that."

"So, where'd you find her?" I asked.

"The doc's body was found a hundred yards off of the most popular run into Bear Valley. Right under our noses! I couldn't fucking believe it. Even if she was buried up to her neck, somebody would've heard her calling for help."

Phil drained his beer and crushed the can as he spoke of the doctor. He leaned against the rail and gazed at the lake, quietly for a moment. Then, he said:

"How bout another one?" he asked. I reached into the ice and pulled out another beer. "Here you go."

He took it and popped it open, but he didn't drink for a minute. He just shook his head sadly.

"I couldn't believe we didn't find her," Phil said.

"So, why a homicide, deputy?" I said, taking a beer for myself.

Phil hesitated to answer.

"This thing still bothers me. It stank from the start. Did I mention that Mr. Wong didn't get a room or even stay in the area that night? The day his wife disappeared. I mean, I know he had the kids with him, but...he just left that night. His wife is missing, and he just splits. Can you fucking believe that shit? I wanted to beat his head in."

"Were there vacancies?" I asked.

"Plenty of rooms in Bear Valley. He just drove away like nothing happened." Phil spit into the dirt.

"And what about the insurance company you mentioned," I said.

"It's life insurance," Phil said. "The insurance company is not paying off the policy. They suspect foul play and not an accidental death. That's why they are trying to find me. I was the lead investigator on the case. The insurance company wants to interview me before they payout a quarter of a million dollars."

"Why are you hiding from them?" I asked.

He laughed bitterly, then, he took a long draw from the beer. "Are you kidding? The sheriff wanted it as an accidental death. How can I go tell them something I don't believe? My sheriff thought he was fucking, God. He ordered me to investigate it as an accidental death or else."

"Phil, did you see the corpse?" I said.

"Sure did."

"Decomposed?" I said.

"Definitely," Phil said, "and the body was dismembered. The

head was separated, as were the arms and the left leg. Just about all of her flesh was gone. The elements, weather, animals, and everything else got to the body."

"Must have been tough figuring out the cause of death," I said.

"Exact cause of death, yes," Phil said, "but it was a homicide as sure as I'm standing here."

"Why?"

"Let me back up a little," Phil said, "So, I was notified first when the body was found that June. I was off-duty when dispatch paged me. All they said, was a body was discovered on the mountain. I knew it was the doctor. But, by the time I arrived, every asshole and his brother had stomped through my crime scene. They even removed the body. I was the coroner on call and this was my body and my crime scene. I was fucking livid."

"Who gave the order to remove the body?" I asked.

"The sheriff. They bagged the body and moved her to the sheriff's office immediately."

"Go on," I said.

"You know, the sheriff said the doctor was killed by a bear or cougar. The idiot also mentioned coyotes as a possibility. Any dumb ass would know that a bear, a cougar, and, especially, a coyote, would be so scared of a skier slicing downhill, they'd run away in a heartbeat."

"O.K.," I said. "So, what made you think it wasn't a wild animal?"

He ran his fingers through his thin hair. Then, he went on. "Doctor Wong's neck was cut clean; I mean with a sharp blade. It was not chewed off. It was sliced through between cervical five and six vertebrae. Her neck vertebrae had been chewed, but the separation below the skull was perfect. She was decapitated, man. There were serration cuts from the knife on the bone."

"Jesus Christ!" I exclaimed.

We both just stood there for a minute. Finally, I said, "So Phil, who found her on June 8?"

"I'm not sure. I never got a straight answer. Some say it was a mountain biker, and others believe a hiker stumbled onto her. The caller was anonymous."

Why "anonymous," I wondered. Then, I asked, "Did you take a

look at the crime scene?"

"Sure I did. After examining the body and arguing with the sheriff, I hightailed down there. Most of the skeleton, the torso had been located under a pine tree. What I noticed and what nobody else did, was a bed made of branches and twigs under that tree. No way an animal made that. It was manmade."

"Sounds as if someone made themselves comfortable. A preparation for an attack, sexual assault or rape?"

"Bingo!" Phil exclaimed. "Absolutely and that's what happened. The fucking explanation for this from my boss was that Doctor Wong was tired and made herself comfortable. She fell asleep and was killed by a bear or something. Doctor Wong didn't make a bed of twigs so she could take a nap. She was less than a hundred yards from the bottom of the run. The fucking thing stinks."

Why, I wondered, would Dr. Wong stop, make a nest, and take a nap near the bottom of a ski run? It was ridiculous.

"So Phil, who did this?" I said.

"I know about the case you were working on. I know about the guy you caught: Paul Candler. He lived close enough, and he's bad enough."

"That's what I'm thinking," I said.

We ambled around his Cherokee as we thought it through. Then, we both leaned against the hood and looked at the lake.

"At first, I liked the husband," He went on. "And, of course, we always look at who's closest to the victim and who benefits. He had a healthy life insurance policy on his wife. I thought that a hit-for-hire might be his cup of tea."

I thought it over. Golden Rule number one in crime: Follow the money. Phil paused for some beer. Then, he went on, "The husband had no blood or scratches on him. He was a doctor, too. A skinny little guy. He didn't do it himself. I looked into gambling debts, consumer debts, drug habits . . . I came up with nothing. I'd say he wanted to get rid of the wife. Shit, their home's worth a cool million."

Phil kicked at the dirt again. Then, he said, "The fact is, I'm convinced she was murdered, and it wasn't random. The Doc was selected."

Phil had only been with Alpine County for two years, but, prior to that, he served eleven years with the Los Angeles Police

Department. This was not his first homicide investigation; it was number twenty-three.

Phil knew what he was talking about. He had no doubts as to the fate of Doctor Katherine Wong, and, now, neither did I.

The way I saw it, Paul Candler must have spilled the beans to the FBI the day we caught him, turning over a body 2,400 miles away at a ski resort in California. In exchange, the FBI made sure the Alpine County Sheriff came up with a good story.

The last thing the Yosemite investigation needed was a monkey wrench tossed into the works. The FBI didn't want the public to think they'd (FBI) lost control and that the Yosemite killer remained at large.

Additionally, Mt. Reba (Bear Valley) is the largest single tax contributor in Alpine County. If Dr. Katherine Wong was murdered or the death was suspicious and publicized as such, it might have bankrupted the county. In return, the sheriff would be getting a night watchman's job. The kibosh was put on the media, and families skied that winter.

As for Deputy Phil, the sheriff directed him to close the case immediately as an accidental death by an animal. Sure, it was probably an animal that killed Doctor Katherine Wong, but this one had two legs.

Two weeks later, Deputy Phil was fired. The FBI saved face, the Bear Valley ski resort saved face, and the Alpine County Sheriff's Department saved face.

But, for Dr. Katherine Wong, wife and mother, there was no closure, no certainty, and a lot of strange coincidences.

Candler was in Tehachapi for the time being, and that was a good thing.

Location of *Dr. Wong's* Body & Route the Killer Drove

Map is not to Scale
Drawn by Stephen M. Sanzeri

CHAPTER 26

March 2001
Murphys, California

"WALKS LIKE AN APE"

PRESS COVERAGE OF the Yosemite Sightseer Case slowed up after Cary Stayner's federal murder indictment. Investigators weren't saying anything about the State's upcoming case in the murders of Carole, Juli and Silvina. Cary Stayner confessed to murdering all four women, and the FBI believed him.

Almost everyone believed him. Except for me. But I wasn't alone.

Many people believed that Cary Stayner could not and did not act alone. These were not only everyday folks—neighbors, community members, snitches, and tweakers, but also law enforcement with connections close to the investigation.

The media didn't buy the lone killer theory, questioning Stayner's ability to control and murder three women by himself. The families expressed concern that they did not have all the facts of the murders. They wanted to know what really happened.

Jens Sund, Carole Sund's husband and the father of Juli Sund initiated a civil litigation against the Cedar Lodge. The Pelosso family initiated their own lawsuit, and for the same reasons. They wanted to be sure that Stayner could not profit from his story, but they also wanted more information about the killings, while holding Stayner and the Cedar Lodge responsible for the deaths.

As the State's murder case against Cary Stayner was about to begin, I came across a *Modesto Bee* story that was published back on June 27, 1999. Reporter Mike Mooney had interviewed a witness in the Yosemite case named Rhonda Dunn.

Ms. Dunn stated that she saw some strange men hanging around the Cedar Lodge back in July of 1998, while she and her mother were vacationing in the Yosemite area.

She described one of the men who were stalking her, and, when

99

I read her account, it sounded as if she was describing, Paul Candler.

Under oath, Rhonda said that the "stalker," Cary Stayner, was with three other men. Rhonda and her mother were so fearful that they checked out of the Cedar Lodge the following morning, three days earlier than originally planned.

Dunn's incident at the lodge wasn't the only one reported. There were other stories about Cary Stayner stalking women around the lodge. It appeared that Stayner had a bad habit of entering hotel rooms occupied by females.

And he was not alone.

Another interesting note is that Joie Armstrong used to party with her friends at the Cedar Lodge. The bar was one of the very few watering holes in the area, so everyone, from off-duty park rangers, biologists, bikers, tweakers, parolees, ex-cons and professionals – hung out there. The chances that Stayner and his buddies had seen her in the only restaurant/lounge for miles around were very high.

The creeps who worked at the Cedar Lodge included: Darrell Gray Stephens, Billy Joe Strange, and, of course, Cary Stayner.

On March 27, 2001, I placed a call to Zach Zwerdling, the attorney for the Sund family. I explained my findings, my investigation, and my interest in the case. Zwerdling welcomed my information because he was also skeptical about Cary Stayner as the lone killer. He suggested I speak to Rhonda Dunn.

I called her right away. After brief introductions, I got into it. I asked her to describe the men.

"One of them walked like an ape or a gorilla. He walked like that guy…what was his name? Oh, yeah…he walked like "Cornelius" in the movie, *Planet of the Apes*? He was hanging around with the other creeps."

"What about tattoos?" I asked.

"Both arms; get me a photo and I'll tell you if it's him."

"No problem. But, tell me about the ink on his arms."

"There was a devil tattoo on his right forearm," Rhonda said, pausing to think. "It was a devil tattoo that's for sure. Maybe a she-devil. He also had a big picture on one arm and a spider web on his elbow. He was scary looking. That's for sure."

Rhonda paused a moment as she relived the moment. I could almost feel her shuddering through the phone. Then, she went on.

"He looked right at me."

"O.K.," I said, "So, what about Stayner?"

"Oh yes, he was there too," Rhonda said.

"You're sure?" I said.

"He had a weird stare I'll never forget. And when I saw his mug shot on TV, I freaked out." Then, she added, "I phoned the FBI."

"I didn't know that," I said.

"Yeah, after I saw Stayner on TV, I called the FBI, but, it was weird. They kind of kissed me off. They told me I didn't know what I was talking about. Then, right after Mike Mooney interviewed me, the FBI paid me a visit. They didn't really say much. I told them what I said to Mooney."

"No shit."

We both fell silent.

"Listen, Rhonda, I'm going to send you some photos. Call me if you recognize any of the men, OK?"

"Sure, no problem. If it helps put these assholes away, I'm fully on board."

After we hung up, I contemplated what she'd told me. I came away with the fact that I believed her. She'd seen Candler and Cary Stayner together at the Cedar Lodge. (Also known locally as "Speeder Lodge.")

I put together a photo lineup of six photographs, including Candler's bail photo. The other five pictures were previously bailed clients who looked similar. I sent them off to her.

Four days later, Rhonda called.

"It's five . . . number five!" Rhonda said excitedly. "He's the one I saw with Stayner and the others. Is that Paul Candler?"

Her certainty sent a thrill of excitement through me. I knew there had to be a connection between Candler and Stayner at the Cedar Lodge. And the others? They had to be Larwick and Dykes.

"Number five?" I said. "You sure?"

"Number five. He had the tattoos."

"Rhonda, you've got to be sure about this," I said.

She interrupted me. "Oh, it's him all right. I'm positive. He scared me, and I don't forget people who scare me."

This was a huge break. I had a witness who could put Cary Stayner with Paul Candler, but who could I tell?

CHAPTER 27

April 15, 2001
Eureka, California

"MY BIG MOVE"

ON APRIL 15, 2001, I faxed an 18 page report to Mr. Angell, the Attorney for Francis and Carole Carrington. Two hours later, Mr. Angell responded and thanked me. He forwarded the report to Francis Carrington.

An hour later the phone rang. I looked at the caller ID and it read, "Francis Carrington Co." I took a couple deep breaths. I didn't expect a response so quickly, if at all. I was about to talk with a man who'd lost his daughter and his granddaughter, victims to horrific deaths.

I'd never worked a case so tragic. I wasn't sure how to handle talking to someone who'd experienced such a terrible loss. On the fourth ring I picked up the phone and answered.

"Mr. Sanzeri, this is Francis Carrington. I received your report, and I found it very interesting."

"Thank you, sir."

"Thank you. You have found some compelling information."

Carrington went on to explain that he was aware of Paul Candler and the arrest I'd made in Fultondale, Alabama.

"Do you mind if I call you Stephen?" he asked politely.

"No, not at all. You can call me Steve." I answered.

"All right then. I checked you out, Steve. The Chief of Police in Fultondale is a personal friend of mine. He told me that you were in a sticky situation with Candler, and that you'd handled yourself very well."

"Thank you, sir."

Mr. Carrington went on to tell me that he owned a shopping center in Fultondale, Alabama.

"I have to tell you," Francis said. "It's very strange. You arrested Candler in a town where I own a strip-mall."

What in the hell was Candler doing in the same town as a

Carrington-owned investment? I wondered. Candler could have run and hid in any town. I don't believe in coincidences. There was something peculiar about Candler moving to Alabama, twice.

Francis Carrington seemed like a smart and articulate man. He'd been dealing with the FBI and investigators for over two years, and he knew something wasn't right with the case. The family never thought Cary Stayner acted alone, and they still didn't. He was particularly interested in the Candler connection.

Before I hung up, I promised Mr. Carrington that I would stay in touch and update him with new information as I received it. He thanked me. He said that it was people like me, who helped the family through their grief by searching for the truth.

I was back in business.

CHAPTER 28

April 2001
Mariposa County, California

"MARIPOSA MESS"

THE LEADING PROSECUTING agency in the Yosemite murder case was Mariposa County. I thought how much it would help my investigation if I could talk with those guys. Problem was I had a history with Mariposa County—a bad history. No way in hell we'd sit down for a friendly cup of coffee.

Back in 1995, they'd set me up in a situation that could have gotten me killed. Oh yes, the Mariposa County Sheriff's Office and I had a past like a bad marriage. This put my investigation of the Yosemite case and me in a tough spot. But, I was willing to tango with these guys again, because I had a strong motivation. My incentive resulted from the suffering of the victims and their families' grief.

Many people were convinced that Stayner did not act alone. His story had holes big enough to drive a semi through them. If he had help — and I was confident that he did — those dirt-bags deserved to be caught and punished.

To the public, it looked like the FBI and Mariposa County got their man. Slam-dunk! Everybody can go home. These law enforcement agencies didn't want to stir up trouble or risk muddying the case against Stayner. They had Stayner's confession. And even if there were inconsistencies, it was a slam-dunk. Good job well done.

But, it wasn't a slam-dunk to me. If anyone deserved justice, it was the victims and their families, the Carringtons, the Sunds, and the Pelossos. Hell, I'd want the same for my family. But, I was going to have trouble with Mariposa, because I'd had trouble with them before.

It was June of '95 and I was chasing the main drug mule for the

Mariposa County Sheriff's Department. If you think I'm kidding, check out *The Last Circle* by Cheri Seymour.

In the first chapter, she mentions the 1980 drowning death of Mariposa County Deputy Ron Van Meter.

Ten years later, his torso washed ashore, dragging various weights that included a fire extinguisher.

The investigation of his murder led straight to the doorstep of MCA Corporation (Music Corporation of America), parent company to Curry Company, the largest concessionaire in Yosemite National Park.

Curry Company operated a major drug network, based in the park, compelling Park Ranger, Paul Berkowitz, to go before the House Interior Subcommittee on National Parks and Recreation to testify about drug distribution by Curry Company officials.

One investigator discovered Sheriff's deputies unloading drugs on a regular basis at the Mariposa airport.

So, when I say I was chasing the main drug mule for the Mariposa Sheriff's Department, I wasn't kidding. His name was Cliff Watkins, and he had a felony bench warrant for jumping on Wyckoff Bail Bonds, out of Twain Harte. I was retained to find Mr. Watkins.

After a few trips to Mariposa County, the Sheriff's Department arrested me for felonious battery, trespassing, and brandishing a weapon. I beat the case, because what they arrested me for never happened. District Attorney, Christine Johnson was pissed.

You see, each time I came to Mariposa County looking for Cliff Watkins, the Sheriff's Department would notify Watkins that I was in town. I found out later that the first time I hit Cliff's house, he was standing behind the door with a .40 caliber. Maybe I had an angel on my shoulder, but, for some reason, I chose not to enter that night.

I had some serious charges, charges that could result in prison time. The peculiar thing is that I was never booked into jail. Even so, the case went to a preliminary hearing, but the story of my arrest never even hit the local paper and cannot be found on the Internet.

Are you fucking kidding? Bounty hunter arrested in town of 2,500 people and no ink? Even a kid who breaks a window gets written up in the daily crime reports.

Mariposa County and their vindictive little District Attorney covered this up pretty good. State prison had been their plan for me five years earlier. But they lost their case against me, because there was no case!

Still, Mariposa had a bad taste in their mouths where I was concerned. And, given their tendency to dispose of people that crossed them, I wasn't too eager to contact them.

But, after I thought it over, I knew that what I was doing for the Carrington, Sund and the Pelosso families' was worth facing Mariposa and their bullshit. I could survive another bout with Christine Johnson and Co. But, the only way I'd go to bed with Mariposa County this time was with me on the top. They'd already tried to fuck me in the ass, but that wasn't going to happen again.

I explained the situation to my attorney and good friend, Larry Murray. He was adamant. He told me that I shouldn't even consider diving back in with Mariposa for the Yosemite case. Larry was one of my two defense attorneys when I was indicted in Mariposa. He was well aware of how they played ball. But, after I explained why it was so important, he told me he would be there for me if I got into some shit.

It's good to know someone's got your back.

CHAPTER 29

April 2001
Lake Don Pedro, California

"ORB HATTON"

I WAS CONSIDERING how I could approach Mariposa, when I remembered what Barbara Dobbins had said down in Alabama, back in June of 1999. We were standing in her bedroom and she was sobbing.

"Paul made me run away from you guys", Barbara said. "He makes me do a lot of things."

Then she mentioned Orb Hatton.

But, why did Candler think Orb Hatton, a former Modesto PD narcotics officer, was after him? I decided to find out. I had some connections there, so I called my good friend, Sergeant Ron Cloward.

"Orb Hatton?" Sergeant Cloward asked, "Shit, he's a good old boy."

"Was he a good cop, Ron?"

Ron was quick to answer, "The best there is!"

Orb Hatton had been a cop for twenty-two years, with fifteen of those in narco. He retired and now owned a real estate company based in Tuolumne County.

On April 30, 2001, I contacted Orb Hatton. As with Deputy "Phil," Hatton would not talk on the phone, so he agreed to meet me at a parking lot next to Lake Don Pedro.

Hatton didn't waste any time and got right to the point. "Not a lot of people know what I'm about to tell you," he said, chewing on the end of a cigar. He was a big man, but he carried his weight well. His hair was still full with traces of gray, and his eyes were as bright and shrewd as a Marine sharpshooter.

"Look, Sanzeri, I know what you're trying to do. I fell into a similar situation back in the mid '80s. I called it the Mariposa

Mess."

I felt a jolt; my own Mariposa County experience had been a mess, too. He went on, squinting out over the lake. "I got mixed up in the shit up there. From what I've heard, sounds like you've stepped in it, too."

"Barbara Dobbins mentioned your name to us down in Alabama," I said.

"Not surprised," he said, and he coughed a little. "I read about you nailing Candler. Sounds like you might be lucky to be alive, after trying to grab that fuck'n punk."

He paused and frowned. "That son of a bitch tried to kill me."

"That was the firearm charge I bailed him on?" I asked.

"Yeah, and he had a weapon all right."

"What happened?" I asked.

"It was back in November 1998 on the 20th," he began. "Candler came to my real estate office and confronted Mary, my secretary. He demanded to see me, and made her phone me in Modesto. The fucking asshole was aggressive, and she was scared to death." He chuckled without humor at the memory. "That guy's scary, ain't he?"

I nodded in agreement. "Oh, yeah."

"Well,' Hatton continued, "Candler said he wanted to kill me. I couldn't fucking believe it. He wanted a meeting so he could do just that!"

"Must've been loaded, too," I said.

"Well, you gotta be crazy and high to walk into somebody's office and demand a meeting so you can kill him!" he said. "And, here's the kicker."

He paused to relight his cigar. "I had no idea who the hell Paul Candler was."

"No shit!" I said.

"No shit is right. I found out later, he was Barbara Dobbins' boyfriend, but I'd never met him. And, I only met Barbara a few times."

Orb Hatton hit on his cigar. Then, he continued, "Yeah, Barbara Dobbins is another piece of work. Looks pretty good on the outside, but, inside, she's as rotten as he is."

"What do you mean," I asked.

He shot out a smoke ring. "She worked for my partner as a part

108

time secretary for a few months. He fired her for some missing checks she couldn't explain. At first, I thought that's what Candler was all pissed off about." He paused to consider his cigar. Then, he looked at me with those shrewd eyes. "But, it wasn't about firing his girlfriend."

"What in the hell was it about?" I asked.

"It was about the 'Mariposa Mess,' and their corrupt Sheriff's Department and D.A. It was about the things I did up there years ago. But let me finish about Candler."

I didn't say anything; I just waited for him to continue. The tight feeling in my guts was now a familiar sensation; I felt it every time I discovered a new angle in this case.

Hatton went on. "Candler yammered something about killing me over the phone in my office. Shit, I was worried about Mary. I took off like a bat out of hell, and arrived in less than an hour. By then, Mary was gone. The office was locked."

"Shit, did he take her?" I asked.

"That was my first thought, but Mary called the office when I got there. She was upset, and she did the right thing: she got out of there. That fucking punk threatened her." He chewed his cigar fiercely. "Yeah, it takes a real man to threaten a woman, doesn't it, Sanzeri?"

I could only shake my head, fascinated by his story.

He went on. "Mary told me that Candler wanted to meet with me at the intersection of Highway 132 and Piney Drive, outside Sonora. He was driving a blue Toyota truck."

"So, you met with him?" I asked.

"I sure did," Hatton said. "Looking back, it should've been against my better judgment to meet with the asshole. But, I was hot at how he'd scared the shit out of my secretary, and I was hot about a man who said he wanted to meet with me, so he could kill me."

I looked at Orb Hatton. He didn't look like a man you'd want to tangle with.

"He was parked in the dirt at the turnout," Orb said. "And he gets out of his truck with a handgun. I pulled my weapon and drew down on him. I told him three times to drop it. He told me to fuck off and started to raise his weapon. I was just starting to squeeze, when all of sudden, Candler gets back in his truck and takes off like a maniac. He was all over the road."

He shrugged, "Fuckin tweakers."

"What happened next?" I asked, enthralled by the story.

"I chased him for a mile or so. He pointed his gun out the window a few times, but never popped a round at me."

Hatton started to laugh. The sound came from deep inside his belly and rose to his mouth. "Ha! Then the dumb shit rolled his truck!"

He shook with laughter, waving his cigar at Candler's stupidity.

"I walked up and grabbed his gun, a nine-millimeter Berretta. I dragged him out and used my belt to tie his hands. Candler was bloody as hell."

"That's fuckin amazing," I said. I shook my head in disbelief. What a crazy son of a bitch!

Hatton went on. "You know what was really fucked; his ten-year-old son was with him." Whatever smile he had on his face faded abruptly.

"Got to be kidding," I said. "Was the kid hurt?"

"Not bad at all, thank God," Orb said. "He went to the hospital, had a broken finger."

He sighed. We both contemplated the part about the children who are caught up in their parent's shit.

Then, Hatton went on, "You know what really bent me, Sanzeri?"

I shook my head.

"The chicken shit D.A. didn't charge Candler with child endangerment."

"It's always the kids who pay, isn't it?" I said.

"Ain't it the truth," he commented.

"So, why the ambush?" I asked.

"It's simple, man. I knew Candler ran dope for Mariposa, and I suspect he did hits for hire. He's been protected by the Mariposa Sheriff, the Mariposa D.A., and by Tuolumne County."

I thought of Sumiton, Alabama, the hit-for-hire capital of the country. Candler picked that exact spot to run to. I remembered the NCIC problem in Alabama. The cops down there had told me he wasn't in the system. Then, suddenly, he was. I recalled the vanishing warrants that Atwater Captain Petro described to me. Poof! I thought about the attack on my partner.

Candler was a guy who did what he wanted with impunity. The whole thing stank like hell. I looked at Orb Hatton. He seemed like a good man. Then, I asked him about his adventures in the same county that tried to hang me. Mariposa.

"Well," he said, puffing on the stogie. "It was back in 1984, and I'd been secretly contracted by the newly elected Sheriff of Mariposa County to look into department corruption and the death of Deputy Ron Van Meter. You know about Van Meter's death?"

"Yes sir, I do," I said.

"I had two partners, a former FBI guy and a retired Merced cop, and we were looking into the Van Meter case, when we stepped right into drug activity and that the prior sheriff may have been the drug lord. There were a lot of deputies left around from the old administration, and we trusted no one. I worked the assignment for six months, until Sheriff Mattheys, was asked to resign. The sheriff was forced out by threats. Nobody wanted to reopen the Van Meter case."

I thought about Van Meter's wife and the devastation she must have felt when his torso was discovered at the lake, wrapped in chains with weights and a fire extinguisher.

Hatton went on, "Basically, Van Meter was a whistle blower. He went to the California Attorney General to report the corruption in Mariposa."

He puffed his cigar contemplating Van Meter's death.

He said, "There was another deputy involved. A guy named Lucky Jordan. Well, he went to the FBI." He smiled briefly, "Yeah, Lucky, was lucky all right. He got witness protection for several years and is still alive."

"Why didn't Ron Van Meter make it?"

"The Attorney General failed Deputy Van Meter," Orb said. "The A.G.'s office contacted Mariposa and told them to investigate their own problems."

"You're fucking kidding!" I said.

"How come you're not dead?"

"I think it's because too many people know about me. They have their own kind of law up there. The minute I stuck my nose in Mariposa, my life's been on the line. This thing is bigger than you may realize. It goes all the way to the top. But, the main reason I'm still breathing is that I talked to the press. The television show, "20/20," arrived in Mariposa to investigate the corruption."

"How did they find out about Mariposa?" I said.

"I called them," Orb said. "The network wanted to break the case wide open after I explained what was going on. But, the producer couldn't get people to talk. And, to top it off, the Sheriff's Department booted the TV crew out of town on the second day!"

"Unbelievable," I said.

"Yup," he said. "The folks in Mariposa are scared."

I could tell Orb was wrapping up. I walked with him to his car. Then, he stopped and looked me in the eye. "Steve, your best friend on this thing is the media. The more people know about what you're doing, the safer you are. Let all your cop buddies know what's going on."

He opened his car door and got in. Then, he looked up at me with his shrewd eyes.

"Let me tell you something: Candler was sent to kill me. It was an ordered hit, but he blew it. The gun charges made good warrants for his arrest. He was going to see a little prison time, but then, he jumped on your bond and ran to Alabama. Twice? Connected is a fucking understatement."

In California, Assault with a Deadly Weapon can earn you between three to 14 years in prison. I thought of Tuolumne County's Assistant D.A. Bill Carlson and his phone call, telling me that Candler was out after serving 30 days. I guess you gotta know the right people.

Hatton closed the door and leaned out. "You told me Candler attacked your partner. That's not surprising. That's the way he operates."

Orb Hatton pointed at me, "Let me tell you something: Tuolumne County is involved with Mariposa. You better watch them all and trust no one."

He started his car. "From what you told me, you are knee deep in this shit." He put his car in gear and looked back at me as he pulled away.

"You better watch your back, Steve."

CHAPTER 30

July 29, 2001
Mariposa County, California

"VINDICATION"

ORB HATTON HAD confirmed my suspicions that Candler was "in" with Mariposa and Tuolumne County law enforcement. The FBI knew about Paul Candler. They knew about his dirty laundry. I wondered what deal he'd made with them. What did he tell them? What kind of a deal did he make with Mariposa? Tuolumne? Calaveras County? Was it about Doctor Wong?

I decided that Hatton was right: get a newspaper guy involved. Mike Mooney at the *Modesto Bee* was my first choice. But, then I thought, don't hide. Go right to the source. Talk to Mariposa County. See what they have to say before I go to the *Bee*. Maybe they would be interested in what I had to say, despite the fact that I was *persona non grata* on their turf.

Maybe my info would help them find the real facts about what happened to Carol and Juli Sund, and Silvina Pelosso. That's what we all wanted, right? The truth?

The case belonged to Mariposa County, and that made me think about Van Meter, the deputy who appeared when they drained Lake McClure; weights and a fire extinguisher chained to what was left of him.

God, what a mess. I wondered if Van Meter was alive when they threw him over board. Or, had they been merciful, killing him before they chucked him into the lake? Either way, it was horrible. Van Meter had been an honest man, trying to do the right thing.

How did that situation fit with me? I'm not saying that I'm a paragon of virtue and morality, but I simply could not walk away. If I could just show enough evidence, maybe the other bad guys would go down. Maybe, just maybe, they would get what they deserved.

I thought about the Sunds, the Pelossos, and the Carringtons. And, I couldn't help but think about Katherine Wong. Was I obsessed? Was I fucking nuts? Whatever I was, with all my faults, my mistakes, and my humanity, those women deserved my best efforts. I would go forward, and I would do my best.

Christine Johnson was still Mariposa's District Attorney. She'd busted my balls before, and I had no expectation that she would make my life any easier now. Getting it together, I called the D.A.'s office the next day.

"We have your file in front of us," Deputy District Attorney, Kim Fletcher said when she answered. "We know who you are."

O.K., I thought, you're ready and waiting for me. Cool. I guess your preparation speaks to your nerves about me.

Mariposa was the lead agency in the deaths of Carole Sund, her daughter, Juli, and Silvina Pelosso. Mariposa had to know about my report to the FBI taskforce. They were certainly familiar with me during their attempt to prosecute me back in 1995 because of a bounty hunt they didn't agree on.

I explained that I had pertinent info on the Yosemite Case. Detective Sarno asked for a meet. Sarno was the lead investigator for Mariposa on the Yosemite case. She was the first to contact Cary Stayner, which eventually led to his arrest. Detective Sarno was the most informed cop on the case.

"I'll meet with you," I said, "but only you."

"I understand," Sarno said. "How about tomorrow?"

"Tomorrow's out for me," I said. "Thursday would be better; Thursday around eleven in Murphys."

"You need to come here," Sarno said.

"I don't think so," I said. "My side of the river, and my partner will also be present."

"We can get a court order," Fletcher said.

"Hey, don't threaten me asshole. I'm not refusing to share information. I called you, remember!"

"Be straight now and fax us what you have right now," Fletcher said. "It's not hard to get a court order, Sanzeri."

"Threaten me one more time counselor and you'll never hear from me again. Maybe I should take what I've got to another agency," I suggested.

"I don't think that's a good idea," Fletcher said. "We are the lead prosecutors in this deal and you need to talk to us first."

"I don't need to talk to you at all!" I said. Shit, maybe this was a mistake." There was silence at the other end. I couldn't hold back, so I laid it out.

"You know what? You guys are so full of shit! I'm calling you to help you, and you can't even get that right!" I felt the anger rise up in my face. "You've got your heads so firmly up your asses; it's just like before, when you filed felony charges on me for nothing."

"Mr. Sanzeri . . . "

"In fact, you set me up! Watkins knew I was coming," My voice rose. "Guess who told him? Guess who set me up?"

"Listen Sanzeri . . ." Fletcher tried to stop me.

"No, you listen, you *knew* I could have been killed. Then, you charged *me* with three felonies to cover your asses!"

"You made a mistake that day," Fletcher said, starting to get excited. "You beat up Jimmy Jones. There were seven witnesses."

"Witnesses?" I said. "Seven dopers? Not one was credible and you knew it. Those motherfuckers were a bunch of scumbags. The only mistake I made was not suing your asses for violating my civil rights."

"You attacked Jones," Fletcher said.

"You can't blame us, Sanzeri. You were in the wrong place at the wrong time" Detective Sarno chimed in.

I could hear pages turning. I took a deep breath. "Look, both of you have short memories," I said. "If you recall, I had a bond forfeiture for Cliff Watkins and was attempting a lawful arrest. He was a dangerous felon." There was no response on the other end. I went on. "Christ, I had a felony warrant and your Sheriff's Department warned him each time I arrived to your little shithole town. What in the hell was that?"

My anger had gotten the better of me. "I found out the truth, you know. I interviewed Cliff Watkins in Shasta County, and he admitted to my investigator that he switched places with Jimmy Jones."

"Mr. Sanzeri," Detective Sarno said, trying to cool things off. "Uh, Steve, let's get back to your information…the reason you're calling." She hesitated. "Why didn't you call us earlier?

"Let me put it to you this way: I didn't call you, because I don't trust you. You protected Watkins, a convicted felon because he moves your dope."

"Mr. Sanzeri," Sarno responded. "What you're saying is serious, and I suggest you back off or get yourself an attorney."

"I've already got an attorney! You met him." I was hot now. "Watkins *told* me he was ready to shoot me the first time I went to his apartment. He *told* me the Sheriff's Department called him and told him I was on my way. I was a dead man."

"We had nothing to do with that. We're not going to discuss it with you. That case is over," Fletcher added carefully.

"You cost me twenty-five grand for my defense," I said, not willing to let it go.

"Look, that's water under the bridge," Fletcher said.

"Besides," Sarno added. "Watkins is dead."

"Yeah, and that's interesting, isn't it?" I said. "And how did he die...at...what was it? Forty-two-years-old?"

There was no answer.

"You still there?" I asked sarcastically. Shit, what was I doing calling these assholes?

Finally, Fletcher spoke. "Yes, Mr. Sanzeri, we're still here."

Sarno piped up. "We need to see your reports."

So much for any acknowledgement of Cliff Watkins and their setting me up, accusing me of three felonies, and costing me twenty-five grand. I wanted to hang up, but then I thought about Carole, Juli, Silvina and Joie.

"All right. Meet me on the Calaveras side, and I'll hand you copies . . . as many as you want. Just don't fuck with me."

"You have information important to the investigation, and withholding it is a crime," Fletcher said in a prim schoolteacher voice.

By now, I'd had it. "Hey, fuck Thursday – fuck anytime soon. Call me back when you decide to quit playing games."

I hung the phone up gently, and gazed out the window. I felt like I'd just thrown some chum into the water where I was swimming with sharks. The Clifford Watkins case had been an ugly business, and I'd had to fight my way out. I'd sworn I'd never deal with these people again.

And here I was: right back in the shit.

The short, hostile conversation with the "witches of the Mother Lode" reminded me: It was time to cover my ass. Time to call Mike Mooney of the *Modesto Bee*. I picked up the phone.

It was a relief to speak with a real human being, not a representative of a corrupt county with a crooked agenda.

"I'm glad you phoned, Steve," he said.

"It's time for me to talk, Mike," I said, "Off the record on some of it?"

"Fine with me," Mooney said, "so, what do you have?"

Mooney was well aware of the Ron Van Meter murder and Mariposa's dangerous and dirty dope dealings. I described my conversation with Mariposa, including the Cliff Watkins' debacle, a situation he was somewhat aware of.

"Sounds like you better watch your back," Mooney said,

"You're telling me," I said.

"You realize that this is only the beginning," Mooney said. "You're a threat to their investigation, Steve. They don't see you as a helper; they view you as a hindrance."

Mike Mooney was right.

CHAPTER 31

August 13, 2001
Eureka, California

"THE CARRINGTONS"

REDWOOD TREES TOWERED over my car as I drove north on California 101. I was on my way to Eureka, home to Francis and Carole Carrington, Carole Sund's parents, Juli Sund's grandparents. This would be our first meeting.

I was about to meet two folks who'd lost two irreplaceable parts of their lives: their beloved daughter and their equally beloved granddaughter.

During the seven hour drive, I thought about the questions I wanted to ask and the questions I might have to answer. I wanted to hear the Carringtons' thoughts and theories. I also needed to know as much as possible about Carole, Juli and Silvina.

I arrived in Eureka about 7:30 that evening, checked into the Days Inn on Highway 101, and phoned Mr. Carrington. I opened a beer and warmed up the shower, and then there was a knock on my door. I peeped through the observation hole, and there was Francis Carrington.

That was fast. I'd only phoned him 15 minutes earlier. I turned off the shower, opened the door, and offered Francis Carrington a beer.

"Thank you," he said. He looked the same as he had on television: a quiet, dignified man with grey hair, he was soft spoken and polite.

We talked about deer and elk hunting at first. Coincidentally, Francis was hunting in Salmon, Idaho, at the same time I was there during the previous season. Like me, he planned on going again this year.

It was nice having something in common, but it wasn't a cheerful conversation. How could it be? I couldn't help but think that the man in front of me might never want to smile again.

We left the room and walked through the parking lot to a nearby restaurant. Carrington stopped for a moment and looked at me. He wiped his face wearily. Then he said,

"The FBI and Mariposa County have stopped investigating this. They feel you should, too." He looked down at the ground, then back at me. "They have a confession. Why do you want to go on with this?"

I hesitated for a moment. Then, I said, "With all due respect, Mr. Carrington, I honestly feel that Stayner did not act alone. He had help. I know a lot about those bad guys who hung out with him. They're capable of almost anything."

He watched my face as I went on, "It bothers me a lot. I guess you could say I don't like the idea of those bad guys going unpunished."

He sighed, "Well, Steve, neither do I." We walked through the lounge toward the bar. I noticed patrons looking at us. Everyone knew who he was. Most of the locals knew of the Carringtons before the Yosemite case. They were a well-known family. No one tried to speak with him, but I saw a few nods as we strolled alongside candle lit tables.

Francis Carrington continued to talk after we sat down and ordered our drinks.

"Looks like the Mariposa County officials don't want you involved, Steve." He sipped his drink. "I don't think you're too popular down that way."

I smiled back, "Yeah, we don't quite see eye-to-eye, if you know what I mean."

He smiled back at me. "I know all about it. I know more about Mariposa and Yosemite and horrible acts of violence than I ever wanted to know."

He went on, "You offered Kim Fletcher and Detective Sarno your information, and I'm glad. I know you contacted them against your own judgment because you felt that you had to. Thanks for doing that. It was the right thing to do."

I nodded and took a sip of my beer. We were both silent for a moment. "This has had to be hell for you and your family."

"We have our good days and our bad days, Steve."

I didn't know what else to say, so I just mumbled, "I'm so sorry."

"You know," Francis said, changing the subject. "My daughter was a fighter, and she was strong. Stayner would've needed a gun, and there was no gun found."

"Unless he had help," I said.

Carrington went on to express the same emotions many families feel when they have lost their loved ones through horrendous violent acts: frustration. They feel that law enforcement was not being totally honest them.

Carrington frowned. "One thing I've learned is that law enforcement is more interested in protecting their public image than they are in getting at the truth."

"You're right about that," I said. "Mariposa County already has a bad rap. The last thing they want to do is to appear clumsy...like they missed something important."

Carrington looked at me, "I'm no politician, Steve, but you stepped on some toes."

"Some big ones," I replied, "But, if there's a cover up, I'll find it."

Francis Carrington reminded me of the $250,000.00 reward.

"To tell you the truth Mr. Carrington, the reward doesn't motivate me, but the murders of four innocent women does. Of course, it never should have happened. But the way law enforcement has handled the case really pisses me off."

"I agree with you, Steve. The investigation should never have stopped," He choked out the next words. "I still feel that Dykes, Larwick, and Candler were in on it."

"Those are the main three," I agreed.

Francis Carrington knew this thing stank, but he was helpless. His family got the run-around, and they were kept in the dark.

As we finished our drinks, I asked Francis if I could represent the family as their private investigator.

"That has crossed my mind, Steve."

"It wouldn't cost you a dime, sir."

"Money isn't an issue."

"For me, it's personal. I don't like how the cops handled this. And I really don't like those dirt-bags getting away with it."

I could never put my hand out to a family that had lost two loved ones and a dear friend. They'd already paid the ultimate price.

Francis said. "Carole and I would really appreciate your help."

120

"You got it, sir," I said. And then I grinned. "Besides, I'm not finished with Mariposa."

"Just make sure they don't finish you," he said, smiling.

We shook hands and said goodnight with a promise to meet for breakfast the next morning.

When I woke up the next day, I felt drained. Even though I'd never experienced what the Carringtons and the Sunds, had been through, I felt numb from my talk with Francis Carrington the night before. I couldn't remember my dreams, but judging from my feelings when I woke up, they must have been nightmares.

Shaking it off, I jumped into the shower.

Francis and Carole were waiting at the I-Hop a block from my hotel. I greeted Francis, and he introduced me to Carole. Although I was momentarily tongue-tied, Carole made me feel welcome.

I looked into her eyes and wondered how many sleepless nights she'd had. Despite the terrible ordeal, she seemed to possess an inner strength. I took a guess that she was the backbone of the family.

The three of us discussed many of the same things Francis and I'd discussed the night before. Carole agreed with my theory; she was also very certain there was more than one person involved in the murders.

"Francis and I have discussed your offer and we have agreed to hire you," Carole said.

I was flattered, and I thanked both of them.

"Whatever you need," Francis said.

"We just want justice for our girls," Carole said. "We owe it to them."

"I will do my best," I said.

"You've done a lot of work on the case already. We appreciate it," Carole said.

Carole handed me a list of people they wanted me to talk to. Some had already been interviewed by investigators, and I was already familiar with a few of the names.

Somehow, with the Carringtons' behind me, I felt a new strength, a determination to let loose more than ever.

CHAPTER 32

August 14, 2001
Modesto, California

"QUEEN BEE"

I ARRIVED HOME late after meeting with the Carringtons. and my first call went to Nancy Lawson, the name on the top of my list.

Lawson had handed Ms. Carrington a diary at the first vigil, claiming it belonged to one of the women. The Carringtons' wanted to know more about her.

Early the next morning, I popped a call off to Nancy. She was anxious to talk and told me she'd been expecting my call. Nancy had been in contact with the Carringtons since the vigil and wanted to help in any way she could.

Eight o'clock the following evening, I met Nancy at the Acapulco restaurant in Modesto. An attractive woman, she was dressed in tight blue jeans, a short yellow blouse, and white sandals. Her toes were perfectly manicured with no polish.

Nancy sat down in my booth. I wouldn't be human or male if I tried to ignore her slender build and her beautiful large breasts. Yeah, she was a looker.

I could tell she was nervous, so I ordered us a couple of cocktails. After all, they say alcohol is the best truth serum.

I let her get started on her margarita. Then, I got started with the questions.

"So Nancy, tell me about the diary?" I said. "Where did you get it?"

"April Munsen, she gave it to me."

"Who's April Munsen?

"She's a friend who lives in Ceres, just south of Modesto."

"How did April get the diary?"

"She said she got it from Gene," Nancy said.

"Gene?" I said.

"Eugene Dykes," Nancy said. "You know who he is, one of the suspects in the Yosemite murders."

"Yeah, I know who he is," I said.

"April used to buy dope from Gene and then do whatever he wanted." She finished off her margarita and looked around nervously.

"Sex?" I asked.

Nancy tapped the table. "Can I have another drink?" she said.

"Sure," I said, as I signaled the waitress. I changed the subject to something safer.

"When did you get the diary?"

"A week or so after they found Juli Sund at the lake."

Then Nancy told me about the lock of hair.

"I opened the diary and there it was," Nancy said.

"What color?" I asked.

"Brownish Black. I asked April about it, and she told me it was a mistake. I tried to take it, but she grabbed it and threw it in the fireplace."

"Did you ask why she did that?" I said.

"She said it was evidence."

"Evidence in the murders?" I asked.

Nancy looked down for a moment. She swallowed hard and then, she answered. "Yes."

I asked Nancy if there was writing in the diary and she told me there wasn't.

"Let me ask you, Nancy," I said, "why are you so interested in helping?"

I was a little surprised to see that she'd polished off another margarita. She looked at me pleadingly, her empty glass dangling from her long fingers. I took the hint and signaled the waitress.

"Do you have a girlfriend?" she asked suddenly, while we waited.

"Sometimes," I answered, watching her smile at me.

Her drink came, and she sipped nervously, never taking her eyes off my face. Then, she wound her fingers together, and her eyes filled with tears. She clenched her jaw and turned away, whispering. I could barely hear her, but I managed to make out what she was saying.

"I was raped by Gene when I was seventeen," She gulped, and then she twisted the cocktail napkin into a knot. "He forced me to the ground and would not let me up," she continued hoarsely. "Steve, Gene held a sawed-off shotgun to my head."

I reached for her hand. She jerked it away, but then, she brought it back and placed her fingers on my palm. I let them sit there. She smiled up at me through her tears. She wiped her eyes with her other hand, but she kept her other fingers resting on my palm. I touched them reassuringly.

"He raped another girl one week later. I knew her..." Nancy swallowed hard. "Gene took her to the same spot as me. He tried to drown her. She was a sweet kid. Now, she's a real sweet doper." She laughed bitterly, "Yeah, Gene leaves a trail."

"Unbelievable," I said.

"He's a fucking animal."

"He's in prison for a parole violation and not going anywhere for a while," I said quietly.

"Yeah, I know," Nancy said. She pulled her hand away and twisted her napkin some more. "Can I have another drink?"

Great I thought, more truth serum, as I caught the waitress's attention, "Another margarita please."

"Listen, Steve," Nancy spoke urgently. "I need to trust you. No one knows what happened to me."

"Mums the word," I said and smiled reassuringly. "What happened to Dykes after he raped you?"

Nancy lowered her head for a moment and wiped tears from her cheeks.

"Gene, plead guilty to kidnapping and sexual assault of the other girl."

"What about you?" I asked.

Nancy hesitated and looked me in the eyes. "He, plead guilty for sex with a minor. He went to prison. Steve, I know he was involved with the girls' murders at Yosemite. I know it. He could kill easily; he could have done this."

Nancy had been closer to Eugene Dykes than a random victim. I didn't want to pry and upset her more than she was, but I needed all I could get.

"Did you know Gene before he raped you?"

"Yeah, just a little."

"What's a little?" I asked.

"I, I don't really want . . ."

"Nancy, this is tough and I really hate asking personal questions, but I know you want to help. So far, you've done great."

Nancy took a long sip of her margarita, and looked at me with her rich brown eyes. "I'll try, Steve."

"Did you know Gene Dykes prior to raping you?"

"I'd seen him around. He followed me a few times to the store. Empire is a small town. I thought he was an OK guy, at first. We dated a couple of times . . . but, then..." She twirled her glass nervously and gulped. "He held a knife to my throat...he tore my underwear off. Then, he kept hitting me..." Tears streamed down her face.

I'd worked with rape victims before. I knew better than to comfort her by hugging her, but I wished I could hold her in my arms.

Nancy sobbed. "I gave in. I had to or he was going to kill me."

Like many women, she was ashamed she'd let him get away with raping her.

"I'm sorry about this, Nancy," I sipped my drink, thinking of all the women who suffer at the hands of violent men. "Nancy, I think you can help the Carringtons and me get the motherfuckers who killed those girls."

Nancy nodded and took a sip of her margarita. She lit a cigarette. "Do you mind?" Nancy asked, as she exhaled.

"Not at all," I said. I watched her recover her composure while she smoked.

"There's a lot of us who want to help, but we can't deal with the fucking cops," Nancy said. "Some of my friends testified before the Grand Jury. They even took lie detector tests and passed. But, that didn't stop the FBI from harassing them."

"Were you questioned?" I said.

"No, but I don't do dope with those guys. I only drink. I don't hang around those people that much."

"What do you know about Mick Larwick?" I said.

"He's as bad as Gene. He's big into the dope trade around here. Everyone's scared of him."

"Larwick and Dykes are half-brothers, you know this?" I said.

"Everybody knows that. Fuck, they're the worst there is."

"Do you think Larwick is involved?"

"Mick shot that cop in Modesto," Nancy said. "What do you think?"

It looked like I'd found my lead into the central valley dope world. Nancy was just what I'd been looking for. She was my new best friend and if I could keep her sober this thing might work.

Over the next couple of weeks, Nancy introduced me to some of the key players in the central valley meth trade. Nancy fed me names.

She also began to flirt with me, a little touch here, a little touch there. I was careful not to cross the line, and I made sure to give her a six-pack and a joint every so often, and it was working.

Her people began to trust me; they knew I wasn't a threat to anyone's bad habits. Nancy knew I was former cop, but she kept my past employment mum. Info like that could get us both killed, and she understood this.

Nancy knew these people better than I did. We visited trailers, shanties, and the banks of the Stanislaus River under Modesto's 7th Street (troll) Bridge, where crank (crystal meth) was passed around like beer or cigarettes.

I always went there armed, and so were the cranksters. My shape and size helped me avoid anything further than a little pushing match here and there, thank God. Most of them were underweight, but tweakers are usually jumpy. The women are just as dangerous. Their paranoia could guarantee me a dirt nap.

I've seen the aftermath of several homicides due to meth, and they are always extremely violent deaths. No way I was going to be a victim.

I found myself visiting strange out-of-the-way meeting places at 3:00 a.m. It was nerve racking as hell, but the fear honed my senses. I'd pick-up Nancy and drive to some unknown shit hole in the valley where some tweaker said he had information about the murders. Some knew Dykes. Some knew Larwick. And some heard of Candler.

I was in deep, and I planned on hanging around until I found something I could use. Nothing in San Jose's Police Academy prepared me for this.

CHAPTER 33

September 3, 2001
Eureka, California

"MYSTERY CALLER"

I WAS IN with the dopers, so I needed my ass covered more than ever. Nancy was just the ticket to keep my cover cool with these guys.

Mike Mooney knew I was working the underground, so he phoned me every week to check in. With everything I had discovered so far, we both agreed: it was time to bring media attention to my investigation of the case. The *Modesto Bee* would break the story around the first week of September.

No one close to the investigation, including the families and Mike Mooney, believed that Stayner had acted alone. But, the FBI, Mariposa, and Tuolumne law enforcement wanted to cover their asses. That meant that a "slam dunk" confession was better than all the unanswered questions that still hovered in the air.

For me, part of those unanswered questions included bad guys: bad guys who knew the truth about what happened, bad guys who participated in the murders, bad guys who were going to get away with murder.

I phoned Francis Carrington after the *Modesto Bee* interview to tell him the latest. Mr. Carrington knew Mike Mooney; he'd told me how much the family appreciated Mooney's work to expose the truth, to offer another explanation besides the FBI's line about the murders.

"I made a big move with Mike Mooney and the *Bee*," I told him.

"You did the right thing," Francis said. "I trust Mike and I think it's time to open this thing up."

I was real happy to hear this, but I was worried about the family. My relationship with them was private and unofficial. They'd been through hell, and I wanted to spare them as much as possible.

Besides this concern, I was always checking behind my back to see if the Mariposa "law" was loading their slingshots...or their guns for an easy shot at me. I asked Mike not to print anything about me working for the Carringtons, and he agreed.

When I told Mr. Carrington about this arrangement, he said, "I appreciate that. There's no reason for anyone to know what you're doing for us."

"We don't need law enforcement pressuring you or me about the case," I added.

Besides keeping a weather eye on Mariposa for my own sake, I didn't want them sticking their nose in and fucking things up. They'd had their opportunity two months earlier, when I called them to offer information. They'd bailed on following through, so that was on them.

But, now, if Christine Johnson caught wind of my relationship with the Carrington family, she'd bust my balls, or worse, mess with the Carringtons in some way I couldn't control. As I've mentioned before, Mariposa didn't have a lot of affection for yours truly.

"I forgot to mention to you, I received an interesting call from an anonymous law enforcement source," Francis said.

"When?"

"Two days ago."

"Really, they didn't leave a name?" I asked. "How do you know it was a cop?"

"I've been dealing with the police for the last two years. I could tell that the man was law enforcement."

The caller told Francis that Paul Candler was very likely involved with the murders. Francis was a little shocked, but not surprised. He said the caller seemed relaxed, professional, and said things that only a person close to the investigation would know.

"Could it have been an FBI agent?" I said.

"No, I don't think so," Francis said.

I was amazed to learn about the call to Francis implicating Candler. But who in the hell was it and why call now, two years later? Was the "phantom" caller trying to help us or divert us? Was there a snitch out there who was impersonating a cop? Was this a bad joke? I was now thinking some of us might have our phones bugged.

Then, Mr. Carrington told me about another call he received; a very disturbing telephone call from Mariposa County Deputy

District Attorney, Kim Fletcher. Ms. Fletcher insisted that Francis take me off the case. She told him I was interfering with their investigation.

What investigation? I wondered. Mariposa wasn't out there knocking on doors or rolling over dime bag dealers. They'd stopped two years ago. Stayner was caught and they'd quit.

Deputy D.A. Fletcher told Francis Carrington that I was a criminal and a no good son of a bitch. She reminded him of my not so pleasant past with her county, saying I'd broken the neck of a guy named, Jim Jones.

Mr. Carrington set her straight, calmly and firmly. He said he didn't like being told who he could or could not have on this case. With his daughter and his granddaughter brutally killed, there was no one getting in his way when it came to solving the murders.

"Ms. Fletcher called me late yesterday. She acted as though it was personal between you two," Francis told me.

"I guess in some ways it is," I said.

"I don't understand it," he went on. "It's as if they're against us—the victims' families." He sighed, "I felt this way from the beginning. No one has been straight with us."

I heard Carrington stop for a moment. It sounded as if he was talking with his wife, Carol. Then he came back on.

"You keep doing what you're doing, Steve, and don't worry about it. I'll call Mr. Angel."

Deputy District Attorney Kim Fletcher showed no class jumping all over Francis Carrington. By attacking me and my participation in the case, Fletcher had only succeeded in making Mariposa law enforcement look even worse than it had first appeared.

The phone call to Francis was Mariposa's attempt to stop me from doing what they refused to do: find out what the hell really happened at Yosemite, what really happened to those women. Or, maybe, they already knew what had happened, and they were covering their asses.

This situation would continue to bother me, especially when only a month later, Tuolumne District Attorney Nina Deane took an early retirement. Six months into her second elected term, in the middle of the biggest homicide of her career, Deane suddenly decides it's time to retire, time to sail away into the sunset with her husband. I don't believe in coincidences, and I certainly didn't believe that Deane had a sudden attack of change-your-life without a good reason.

As for Mariposa, whatever they were doing, they were worried about me, worried enough to call Carrington directly.

"Keep your enemies' - enemies closer." I believe this. I stepped into the arena knowing perfectly well what could happen and so far I was dead-on. I'm not a glutton for punishment and I don't mind a fierce foe, but let's try to keep it halfway fucking fair.

Most bounty hunters are part renegade. After Mariposa County dragged me through the shit back in '95 that renegade part of me grew a ton.

Earlier in my life, I took an oath to protect and serve the constitution and sovereignty of the United States of America. That was when Burlingame Police Chief Fred Palmer handed me my badge. I believed in my oath, and I never gave it up.

But, now, all that I believed in, all that I thought was good and decent had become blackened. The Mariposa incident had toughened me up, and now they were going to face the Frankenstein Monster they'd created.

I would be using the whole enchilada on this one . . . no holds barred. I just needed to survive a second round with those devils.

CHAPTER 34

September 4, 2001
Murphys, California

"WHO'S ON TOP NOW?"

I WAS SITTING at my desk, completing the paperwork for a five-thousand dollar bail bond. Just after 2:00, the phone rang. Mariposa Sheriff's Detective, Cathy Sarno was on the line, and, to my surprise, she wanted to meet.

My first ball bashing session with her and Deputy D.A. Fletcher had left me skittish. Then, after Fletcher's phone call to Mr. Carrington, dissing me and my reputation, I never expected Mariposa to come crawling back.

I was confused.

"Why the sudden change of heart?" I asked.

"What do you mean?" she replied.

"You and Fletcher gave me hell when I called a few months back. And, then, Fletcher phones Carrington, telling him I'm a 'no good son of a bitch.' Then, she practically calls me a criminal."

I paused for a breath, then, I continued, "You and I both know the real story. Now, what was all that horseshit about?"

I didn't expect an immediate or truthful answer. The line was silent.

"Are you still there?" I said.

After a pause, Sarno said, "Yes."

"And?" I asked.

"Why didn't you come forward earlier?" she asked.

"Ask the FBI," I said. "The taskforce got my report eighteen months ago."

"See, that's just it, Sanzeri, you don't play by the rules." Sarno said, getting a little hot, "You stepped over us to get to the Feds, and it was our case."

"Did you read my report?"

I could feel her hesitate, then, she said, "No, I haven't seen it."

"O.K.," I said. "Let's start over. What do you want exactly?"

"I want to know more about Paul Candler and his girlfriend, Barbara Dobbins."

There it was. After all this time, someone wanted to know more about what I had on Candler. Amazing.

"I hate talking over the phone, detective. Hasn't seemed to work for me lately. Let's meet." We made a date for September 6, at 10:00 a.m. Strange, I thought, Detective Sarno was unaware of my reports to the FBI taskforce. No wonder this case was a mess.

September 6 arrived. Rick and I had scripted our story, and we were on the same page. The timing for the Mariposa meet was perfect. And even better, although Sarno would not know it, Candler's name was about to hit the *Modesto Bee*.

I was in my office setting a "bug," a hidden mic in my penholder. Wireless, it would transmit to the tape recorder in the garbage can under my desk.

Rick arrived with a bag of freshly baked donuts.

"Smells good," I said,

"All wired up?" Rick asked.

I stuffed a donut in my mouth and showed Rick the setup.

"I'll go first," Rick said.

"I need to go first," I said with a mouthful of banana crème. "I need you to monitor. The mic will transmit a hundred feet from here. You should be good in the car."

"O.K.," he said. "I'll wait till she shows."

A few minutes later, we watched as a brown undercover car arrived outside. I went out to meet Detective Sarno. She was wearing a conservative blue skirt and a crisp, white top. With short practical hair, she looked like what she was: an efficient, no nonsense cop.

We shook hands, and I invited her in.

"Donut, detective?" Rick asked, extending the box of pastries to her.

"Thank you," Sarno said, choosing a chocolate covered éclair. She bit into it, her eyes closing briefly with pleasure.

"You know detective," I said. "The statements by Dobbins and Candler made it hard to ignore them or their involvement in the case."

"I'm not sure about that, but you seem to be," Sarno said,

132

reaching for a napkin.

Rick sat on the edge of my desk. "If you were present when Barbara Dobbins and Paul Candler made those statements," he said, "you'd have another indictment."

"You can testify to the statements they made," Sarno said, "but they'll be interpreted by the defense as hearsay."

Rick cleared his throat and glanced at me. "And you know that there are exceptions to the hearsay rule. Spontaneous statements can be the exception."

"Especially when credible witnesses like us are recipients of the statements," I said.

Sarno sat across from me at my desk and wiped her mouth. She smiled briefly and pulled a tape recorder from her purse. She placed it on my desk and switched it on.

Rick smiled as he left the office. "See you in a bit."

Sarno watched him close the door, then she turned to me. "I read your first report to the FBI. You've done a lot since then."

"When did you see the report?" I said.

"I got it two days ago."

"That report is a year and a half old," I said.

"It was a good start," Sarno said. "I wish I'd seen it earlier."

I handed Sarno two copies of the updated report.

"Wow," Sarno said, "how many pages?"

"Thirty-two."

"Anything missing?" Sarno said, as she glanced through the document.

"It's complete," I said.

Sarno turned the pages slowly. I sat back and had another donut, this one filled with raspberry cream.

"This stays between us," Sarno said, looking up.

"I didn't see a problem with that," I said.

I was only with Detective Sarno for about ten minutes. Rick's interview was a few minutes less. She got what she wanted and walked outside to have a cigarette. I joined Rick in the office, closing the door behind.

"How'd it go?" I asked.

"Great," Rick said, "she seems kind of nice."

"Most of the questions were about Alabama," I said. "She also wanted to know about Rhonda Dunn's identification of Candler."

"I think she was surprised at how much information we had."

"Sarno knows a lot more about Candler than I thought," I said.

"I think so," Rick said.

We walked out to meet up with Detective Sarno. She lit another cigarette and leaned against her car.

"I would've gotten to you guys earlier if the FBI hadn't held onto your investigation," Sarno said. "Fucking bothers me."

"O.K.," I said.

"Listen, off the record, I like what you guys are doing," Sarno said. "I think Paul Candler is involved. I didn't think this until recently. That's why we're meeting."

"Candler is in state prison," I said.

"I know," Sarno said. "We can get to him, that's not a problem."

"Do you want him?" Rick asked.

"I don't know if we even want to start this thing rolling," Sarno said. "With Stayner's trial coming up, it could mess everything up."

"We understand," Rick said.

"No statute of limitations on capital crimes," I said. "We have time."

"I want your reports, information, whatever you get, first," Sarno said, "not the FBI. Work with me on that?"

"If we get something, I'll call you," I said.

She smiled briefly, crushed her cigarette under her shoe, got into her car, and drove away.

Rick and I watched her drive away. I know we were both thinking the same thing: Was this going to lead to justice?

The meeting had gone well, but I was still leery of Mariposa's agenda. The egos, politics, corruption, lying, cover-ups, poor judgment, and lousy police work were to blame. The Yosemite Sightseer Murder case was too far gone to fix without a ton of work and a lot of embarrassment.

U.S. Senator Grassley of Iowa had already put a probe up the FBI's ass, regarding the case. He'd also chaired investigations into Waco and Ruby Ridge, so he was the man.

"Next to Waco and Ruby Ridge, the Yosemite Sightseer Murder case is the FBI's third worst blunder," Senator Grassley stated.

I wondered if the Senator was an Ace I could play if I needed to.

CHAPTER 35

September 30, 2001
Modesto, California

"HOT OFF THE PRESS"

ON SEPTEMBER 30, 2001, the *Modesto Bee* ran this story on the front page. I had updated Mike Mooney after the meeting with Detective Sarno, prior to this print.

INVESTIGATOR BELIEVES STAYNER HAD ACCOMPLICE
September 30, 2001 Posted: 06:45:01 AM PD
By MICHAEL G. MOONEY
MODESTO BEE STAFF WRITER

Did Cary Anthony Stayner act alone?

That question is being raised again, as the one-time motel handyman sits behind bars, awaiting trial on charges that he single-handedly and savagely killed three Yosemite sightseers. Stayner, who already has been sentenced to life in prison for the grisly murder of Yosemite naturalist Joie Armstrong, is the only one charged in the February 1999 slayings of Carole Sund, 42, of Eureka, her daughter, Juli, 15, and family friend Silvina Pelosso, 16, of Argentina. But many people, including family and friends of the victims, continue to be convinced that Stayner could not and did not act alone in the brutal killings.

Francis and Carole Carrington, the parents of Carole Sund and grandparents of Juli, have long believed that Stayner had accomplices. "So far," Francis Carrington said Friday, "we haven't been able to pin anything down." But a Calaveras County bounty hunter believes a convicted child molester he tracked down in mid-1999 played a role in the deaths of the Yosemite sightseers.

Stephen Sanzeri of Murphys has told authorities they should take a long look at Paul Leckley Candler Jr. Sanzeri believes Candler was involved in the murders, based on statements he said Candler made to him and private investigator Rick Janes. The pair arrested Candler in June 1999 in Alabama after he jumped bail in Tuolumne County on charges unrelated to the Yosemite slayings.

Since June 2000, Candler has been at the California Correctional Institution at Tehachapi, where he is serving a 17-year sentence for continuous sexual abuse of a 12-year-old.

Candler's name surfaced briefly during the height of the FBI-led investigation, but authorities at that time said they did not consider him a suspect.

But, Rhonda Dunn, a Chicago woman who told *The Bee* last year that Stayner and two or possibly three other men stalked her, has identified Candler as one of those men.

The trio vanished Feb. 15, 1999, from the Cedar Lodge in Mariposa County. They were on an excursion to Yosemite National Park. Their bodies were discovered about a month later at separate locations in neighboring Tuolumne County.

The charred remains of Carole Sund and Pelosso were found in the trunk of their burned-out rental car. Juli Sund's body was discovered on a wooded hillside overlooking Don Pedro Reservoir. Her throat had been slit. Similarities abound for months; the FBI investigation focused on a loosely knit group of drug users and career criminals, and on a number of occasions, authorities announced that they believed the people responsible for the crimes were in custody.

Then, in July 1999, Joie Armstrong was found dead, the victim of a grisly decapitation. The trail led to Stayner, who shocked authorities by telling them he had killed the three sightseers.

Stayner subsequently reached a plea bargain and was sentenced to life in prison for Armstrong's murder. He is awaiting trial in the sightseers' deaths, and, if convicted, could receive the death penalty. Stayner is scheduled to return to court Oct. 29 for a hearing to determine whether the trial should be moved from Mariposa County.

Sanzeri and Janes continued to believe that Stayner did not act alone. They said they tried for months to get law enforcement to listen to their theory about Candler. "Neither one of us know Stayner," Janes said. "But we have talked to people who know him, and they said he couldn't have done it by himself."

No one paid much attention to Sanzeri and Janes until Sept. 6, when they were interviewed by a Mariposa County sheriff's detective assigned to the Sund-Pelosso investigation. Lt. Brian Muller, a spokesman for the Mariposa County Sheriff's Department, confirmed Friday that a detective interviewed the pair. Muller said the investigation remains open and, as a result, he could not comment further on Candler. He did say, however, that information on the possibility of someone else being involved in the Sund-Pelosso murders is being investigated thoroughly.

Sanzeri said the description in *The Bee's* story about Dunn in May 2000 prompted him to contact authorities. Dunn had described being stalked in July 1998. At the time, Dunn, a respiratory therapist, and her mother were staying at Cedar Lodge. Dunn described one of the men she saw with Stayner as 5-foot-6 to 5-foot-7. Sanzeri said Candler stands 5-foot-7 to 5-foot-8. Dunn said the man she saw had medium to long wavy, blond hair.

Sanzeri said Candler has medium-length, wavy, light brown hair. Dunn said the man she saw had an elaborate tattoo on his right forearm with a devil. Sanzeri said Candler has an elaborate tattoo on his right forearm and a she-devil tattoo on his left forearm. Dunn said the man who followed her had a funny walk, almost bowlegged. "He reminded me of Cornelius, one of the characters in the movie 'Planet of the Apes.'"

Sanzeri said Candler is bowlegged. Dunn said the man who followed her was driving an older blue Ford F-150 pickup.

Sanzeri said he and Janes saw an older blue Ford F-150 pickup parked at Candler's former residence in Arnold.

Dunn said she saw the man hanging around Cedar Lodge. She is convinced he was the same man who played "bumper tag" with her car as they drove toward Yosemite. Once in front of her car, Dunn said the man repeatedly sped up and slowed down. She said she eventually passed the pickup and got away.

After reading the newspaper story, Sanzeri contacted Dunn through a Eureka attorney who represents Jens Sund, Carole Sund's husband and Juli's father. Sanzeri said he asked Dunn about the man she saw with Stayner. Dunn was able to pick Candler's picture out of a photo lineup Sanzeri prepared and mailed to her. Sanzeri said no tattoos were visible in any of the pictures Dunn reviewed. In addition, Dunn told Sanzeri that the man she saw was wearing a black T-shirt, blue Levi jeans and cowboy boots.

Sanzeri said Candler was wearing a black T-shirt, Levis and cowboy boots when arrested in Alabama a year later.

Dunn recently told *The Bee* she remains convinced Candler followed her and her mother that day in July 1998. "I'm sure it was him," she said. "He was a lot more aggressive toward me than Stayner."

Candler felt sorry for victims. Sanzeri said he first encountered Candler in November 1998 when he posted two bail bonds for the former Atwater and Modesto resident. Candler's girlfriend at the time, Barbara Dobbins, requested the bonds, Sanzeri said. Attempts to contact Dobbins were unsuccessful.

Sanzeri said Candler had several brushes with the law, including convictions on weapons, drugs and false imprisonment charges.

Two months after the Sund and Pelosso slayings, in April 1999, Candler and Dobbins cancelled their post office boxes in the Tuolumne County community of Moccasin. A short time later, Sanzeri said, Candler jumped bail and the two left the state.

Sanzeri and Janes tracked the couple to Warrior, Ala. As they tried to take them into custody on June 5, 1999, Sanzeri said, the couple sped away in a car with Candler driving.

On June 6, Sanzeri and Janes said they returned to the house and found Dobbins alone. "She was very hysterical," Sanzeri said. "It took us 15 minutes to settle her down for a half-decent conversation." Sanzeri continued: "After she calmed down, I asked her why she and (Candler) had evaded us. (Dobbins) stated to us that (Candler) thought we were the 'feds' and were looking for him regarding the girls that were murdered." Dobbins then told Sanzeri that Candler "felt bad about what happened to the girls."

Sanzeri and Janes said they caught up with Candler on June 7 at a motel. Sanzeri said Candler initially refused to come outside. When Candler came out, Sanzeri said, a scuffle ensued in front of Janes and several police officers who had come to assist with the arrest. Candler was taken to a nearby hospital for treatment of what Sanzeri called "minor injuries." While at the hospital, Janes asked Candler why he ran away. The private investigator said Candler told him he believed Janes and Sanzeri were FBI agents investigating the death of the sightseers.

Janes said Candler told him he felt sorry for the girls.

Investigators believe in theory. Sanzeri and Janes -- who are ex-police officers' -- said the statements by Candler and Dobbins are significant because they were made without any prompting. The investigators said they are willing to take lie-detector tests. Sanzeri said he has only a theory at this point. He has no physical evidence to connect Candler to Stayner, let alone the deaths. Still, he believes Candler -- at the very least -- has information about the killings.

Sanzeri said Candler and Dobbins had been staying in a remote cabin on Grizzly Road -- less than two miles from where Juli Sund's body was discovered.

On Feb. 22, 1999, Sanzeri said, a fire damaged a portion of the cabin. It was about a week after the Yosemite sightseers were seen alive.

I'd just exposed a large part of our investigation and not one phone call from Mariposa or the FBI. I was almost thinking nobody could read. If I were the FBI, I would want to talk to Rick Janes and Stephen Sanzeri, just to see what they were thinking. The only calls generated from the story, were from citizens who recognized Paul Candler's photo.

I received a few, as did the *Modesto Bee*. The story sparked interest and supported the idea that Cary Stayner, had help. The trial was about to start and the prosecution surely did not need a bunch of reasonable doubt clouding Stayner's case.

But, the story radiated with reasonable doubt.

CHAPTER 36

February 2002
Santa Monica, California

"CURVE BALL"

BY NOW, CARY Stayner was as infamous as any murderer in recent years. Stayner's court appointed attorney was nowhere near run of the mill. Marcia Morrissey was equally well known. Ms. Morrissey was out of a big firm in Santa Monica, California, where her claim to fame came from defense cases featuring the Menendez brothers, and Snoop Dogg.

Morrissey was the court's accepted attorney for Cary Stayner in the Federal murder case of Joie Armstrong, and would continue in the same capacity through the State of California's case. Morrissey petitioned for Stayner's defense and he agreed. This often happens in high-profile cases.

As the trial approached, Stayner's defense announced at a press conference in Los Angeles that they were going to present a reasonable doubt defense and bring in other suspects the FBI taskforce arrested.

Now we're talking. I had been waiting for Morrissey's plans to fit into my investigation. It looked as though Stayner's attorney was going to surface Eugene Dykes, Michael Larwick, and possibly the rest of the crew. The statement from Morrissey dropped a bombshell on the prosecution and they scrambled.

The FBI had closed the book two years ago and archived the suspects, and now the Yosemite Sightseer Murder case was being reinvestigated. This was the last thing the prosecution wanted. As for my cause, this was tailor-made. Rick and I had taken Candler as far as we could, but it wasn't over yet, not even close.

Investigators wasted no time retracing their steps. I had messages on my pager via the "snitch network." Cops were shaking down the same dopers as before and getting nowhere. The cranksters had practice. They wouldn't talk to investigators, but they would talk to me.

Mariposa and the FBI had decisions to make. Prosecutors would now have two choices: one, discount Eugene Dykes, Michael Larwick, and anyone else squashing reasonable doubt, or two, build their case with Dykes and company, and slide indictments next to Stayner.

I thought this would be the best idea. The majority of people close to the case believed that Stayner had accomplices; so charging another suspect could be pulled off with less criticism than continuous denial.

Marcia Morrissey was stirring things up, and Mike Mooney was right behind her, as most newspapers suddenly were. Two days after mentioning her defense strategy, Morrissey struck again. Her beef this time, was regarding the 54,000 pages of Discovery. She motioned Santa Clara County Superior Court Judge, Thomas Hastings, for a continuance, and it was denied. Judge Hastings reasons were based on the fact that most of the Discovery was delivered during the federal proceedings and Morrissey should be familiar with it.

February 14, 2002, Valentine's Day, and a day away from the third anniversary of the murders. Mike Mooney decided to write a second story, this time regarding Stayner's defense and naming the original suspects, with Paul Candler as the number one guy to look at. Eugene Dykes and Michael Larwick were also mentioned, but it was all Candler. I phoned Mooney, after reading it.

"Hey, thanks," I said, "that was a surprise for sure."

"It was," Mooney said. "You OK with it?"

"Not a problem; anything to expose our investigation."

"People are talking about Candler, Steve. He's looking better all the time. Did you hear from anyone?"

"Nope," I said, "and that really surprises me."

Mike's second story of our investigation went to press without my knowledge, but I had no problem with it. Seeing Candler's name on the same page as the other two scumbags was a good thing. I couldn't ask for better media support. Then another surprise came four days later, when *The Modesto Bee* revised the second story and ran it again.

142

DID STAYNER ACT ALONE?

February 18, 2002 Posted: 06:30:22 AM PDT
By MICHAEL G. MOONEY
BEE STAFF WRITER

The FBI could not have been more surprised when Cary Anthony Stayner confessed that he -- and he alone -- killed three Yosemite sightseers.

Investigators had been convinced that an intense manhunt had led them to the prime suspects in the 1999 deaths of Carole Sund, 42, of Eureka, daughter Juli, 15, and family friend Silvina Pelosso, 16, of Argentina.

After Stayner confessed, investigators stopped looking for other suspects. But during a hearing in Santa Clara County Superior Court last week, defense attorney Marcia Morrissey said she needed more time to prepare for the trial in the wake of prosecution evidence suggesting that someone other than Stayner killed the Sund's and Pelosso. Morrissey referred to a polygraph examination that she said provided evidence that Stayner might not have been involved in the killings. It was not clear who was the subject of the lie detector test.

Francis and Carole Carrington, Carole Sund's parents, have been working with a Calaveras County bail bondsman to investigate claims that Stayner did not act alone. Stephen Sanzeri, who said he has accepted no money from the Carringtons, said he believes that Paul Leckley Candler Jr. may have been involved. He bases that on statements that he said Candler made to him and private investigator, Rick Janes, when they arrested Candler in June 1999 in Alabama. Candler had jumped bail in Tuolumne County on charges unrelated to the slayings. Sanzeri does not know whether Candler knew Stayner.

Before Stayner surfaced, FBI investigators were preparing to charge Eugene Dykes with the killings. Dykes, now serving a five-year prison sentence on

143

unrelated charges, had confessed to the killings. He recanted that, however, after Stayner's confession. One source close to the investigation previously said that Dykes had been given a lie detector test. During this period, sources said Dykes mentioned a lot of names in connection with the deaths, but never Stayner's.

Until his confession, Stayner had barely made a blip on the radar screens of investigators. He had been questioned, but only because he had been a handyman at the Cedar Lodge, where the Sund's and Pelosso had been staying.

Then, in July 1999, while being questioned about the murder of Yosemite naturalist Joie Armstrong, he made his startling revelation about the Sund and Pelosso killings. Stayner later pleaded guilty to beheading Armstrong and was sentenced to life imprisonment without the possibility of parole.

Today, Stayner sits in a Santa Clara County Jail cell, awaiting a June 10 state trial date. If convicted, the 40-year-old will face the death penalty.

Sanzeri is working to determine if there is any link between Dykes, Stayner and Candler, though sources close to the investigation have said that they know of no connection.

Candler is serving a 17-year prison sentence for repeatedly molesting a 12-year-old girl. Reports circulated in the early days of the investigation that Stayner and others were into "kiddy porn."

Later, Lisa Noe, an Illinois woman who had corresponded with Stayner after his arrest, said Stayner was a pedophile who could only become sexually aroused by prepubescent girls.

Investigators also pursued a story about a group of men, including Dykes, who supposedly held Juli Sund hostage anywhere from a few hours to a few days in the Modesto area.

During that time, she reportedly was drugged and repeatedly sexually assaulted before she was killed.

Investigators never confirmed that story.

Sources have confirmed that fibers in a vehicle that Dykes used matched those from blankets used at the Cedar Lodge. Such blankets, however, are common to many motels and hotels.

Unless someone else comes forward, the mystery surrounding other possible suspects will continue -- at least for now.

When Judge Thomas C. Hastings granted Morrissey's request to delay the trial, he also sealed the legal brief outlining her reasons for seeking the delay.

I was really expecting some heat from the FBI or Mariposa, but again they turned a blind eye and let me be. Three stories and no attention?

CHAPTER 37

February 2002
Murphys, California

"ANOTHER GOOD WITNESS"

I HAVE ALWAYS been a lone wolf; and in my business that's the only way to be. Maintaining a low profile is another good trait, but now that was out the window. I received a call from Nancy Lawson, just after midnight.

"Kind of late," I said.

"I just got back from the liquor store," Nancy said. "You're in the paper again."

"I am," I said.

"I got some calls tonight," Nancy said. "People saw it. Some are freaking out. You said too much."

"Are you on landline?" I said.

"Yes, I'm on the regular phone. Steve, are you listening? Fuck, I'm serious. You need to get down here."

"Hey, take it easy," I said. "How many beers have you had?"

"Fuck, two . . . maybe. That's not what I'm talking about, you're not listening. The fucking cops are really going after people, harassing everyone like they did before."

"Still?" I said.

"Not as bad, but yes. And everyone sure knows who you are now."

"Is anyone talking?"

"They all are. People are saying you're an ex-cop. Some around here might not trust you."

"Anybody say anything about me and the Carringtons?"

"They all did," Nancy said. "That part they liked. I told them I trust you, and that's what matters."

"Do I have anything to worry about?" I asked.

"The ones who wouldn't talk to you before, surely won't now," Nancy said.

"Do me a favor and let me know if somebody has plans. I don't like surprises."

I was a former cop, which was the biggest strike against me. I had entered a lions' lair and tamed the pride, but wild animals are unpredictable and having the cop halo over my head was what would get me ambushed and eaten. I was at the top of my game and motivated with a high, better than the best "ganja." Thanks to Mike Mooney, all the doors were now opened and I wasn't going to hesitate walking through.

Nancy was the Queen Bee and her hive was buzzing. For the most part, she was truthful and a proven commodity. But, ninety-nine percent of the information her doper acquaintances told me was bullshit. A lot of theories, rumors, and tall-tales of what could have happened and what they heard when they were loaded. But, one thing in common was that all of the informants knew Rufus Dykes and/or Mick Larwick.

Rick only accompanied me a couple of times to the valley to meet with Nancy or one of her minions. I kept my partner away most of the time, because together we looked all cop and that would get us nowhere or get us killed. Rick understood this and never complained about a last minute, late night fog soaked drive to Empire or Modesto. He thought that I got too chummy with a few of my moles and he was probably right. The little "bombers" I rolled for my informants was his only bitch.

"Not a smart idea," he told me more than once.

It wasn't simply a great idea for me to do this; it was brilliant. The ex-cop thing was evened out by being an outlaw and passing around a little weed every so often. This icebreaker outweighed any fear of my reputation becoming tarnished or for me going to jail for a day or so. There are no rules when four innocent women are murdered. Being able to walk into a doper's trailer for the first time without a problem was an accomplishment.

As long as the tweakers would talk, I was going to listen. I wasn't as quick to dismiss these people as law enforcement had.

Cary Stayner would be arriving in Santa Clara County Superior Court in about four months. Marcia Morrissey remained steady with plans to expose the original suspects. As for Rick and me, we had a date.

Nancy hooked us up with Ricardo, a former doper who was best pals with Dykes and Larwick. I was interested, and she said he would talk to me. So, we picked up Nancy at her house in Empire, around 9:00 in the evening.

"Let's go," I said to Nancy who was trying to finish her cigarette in the pouring rain.

"All right," Nancy said, as she dropped the cigarette on the wet pavement. Nancy took a seat in the back of the van, opened one of her three beers, and directed us toward the town of Keyes, about four miles away. Rick was his usual, pleasant self, and Nancy warmed up to him a little more than the last time.

"Nancy," Rick said, "is Ricardo for real?"

"He sure is," Nancy said. "Ask Steve. Want a beer?"

"No thanks," Rick said.

It was raining harder when we entered the Safeway parking lot where Ricardo was waiting in his truck. Nancy jumped out of the van and greeted Ricardo with a hug and kiss. I looked at Rick.

"He looks O.K.," I said.

"Nice truck," Rick said, "looks like he might even have a job."

Seemed like a good start. Ricardo sat in the back with Nancy, and drank a beer. We were now en route to Larwick's last residence.

"Mind if I spark one up?" Ricardo said.

I knew Rick would say no, if I let him, so I jumped in and said, "Sure."

Rick gave me the evil eye. "What the fuck?" I smiled.

"So tell us about Larwick?" I said, loudly.

I looked at Rick, as if to say you'll see how it works.

"Want a hit?" Ricardo asked.

"No thanks," I said, "we're O.K. So, how well do you know Larwick?"

"I know Gene a lot better."

Turns out Ricardo went through grade school and high school with Eugene Dykes. Ricardo explained about being interviewed by the FBI. He was questioned about Larwick and Dykes several times. Ricardo owned a small collection of vintage cars that Larwick worked on.

"I've known Mick for twenty years," Ricardo said. "He may be a doper, but he can turn a wrench. Gene does pretty well too."

"So, Ricardo," Rick said, "who's worse to cross?"

148

"I'd say that Gene is crazier than Mick. Mick is more of a drug addict, but Gene is way more violent. Gene is a convicted rapist, you know. They're both the kind of guys you don't want to cross."

"Ricardo, give me a hit of that," I said, as I reached back. Rick looked at me as I took two good tokes, but he knew what I was up to and he played it cool.

"Thanks man," I said, "how much further?" Suddenly, Ricardo got buggy.

"Ya know," he said, looking around nervously. "I don't want to do this anymore. If, Mick fucking finds out, I'm dead. Take me back."

"Larwick's in prison," Rick said, "he won't know."

"Yeah, but he's got neighbors, dude," Ricardo said, "and they all bought dope from him. If we snoop around, he'll find out, I guarantee."

"Look, man, we're not out to get you in trouble. We'll just drive by and take a look," I said. "We're close, where do I turn?"

I waited for an answer.

"Tell them, Ricardo. They're cool," Nancy said. "Tell Steve where to turn."

I could hear his brain turning it over, and he must have decided to trust me because he said, "O.K., fine, but, you guys better not fucking be seen there. I'm not getting out and neither should you."

It was after 10:00 p.m. when we arrived in Larwick's old neighborhood, and Ricardo pointed out the corner house. What a dump. The place was dilapidated and looked abandoned, and I'm sure it was. Dark and raining, with a lot of overgrown bushes, it would be easy to sneak in for a look. Ricardo leaned in between Rick and me, and pointed.

"That's where Mick kept his Camaro," Ricardo said, "in that detached garage. I told the FBI that when they took me here."

"How in the hell did the FBI find you?" Rick asked.

"I dropped my cars here for Mick to wrench on them. Sometimes, Mick would work on my cars at Larry Utley's house. After Mick was arrested for shooting that cop, the FBI went to Larry's. They checked the license plates on the cars in the backyard and two were mine, so I got a visit."

"What happened to Utley?" I said.

"They arrested Larry when he tried to run out the backyard," He laughed suddenly. "He was naked, man!"

"So what happened next?" Rick said.

"Utley violated his parole, so they took him." Ricardo started to warm up to his story. "Then, when the FBI started talking to me, I took them to Mick's house and told them what I knew. That's it."

"Did the FBI know about Larwick's house before you told them?" Rick said.

"I think I was the first person to show them this place. They were surprised and even thankful. They acted like I was some kind of hero. They bought me lunch, brought me beer sometimes, and even showed up at my home just to say hello. Then, it was weird. I never heard from them again."

I understood why Ricardo was so nervous. He was the first person to turn investigators on to Larwick's hideout. Although Larwick and Dykes were in prison, Ricardo's fear heightened the longer we stayed. Our tour guide was anxious to leave.

"Let's get out of here, man," Ricardo said. "You've seen the place."

"We're not ready yet," Rick said, "we need to know what you told the feds."

Ricardo asked Nancy to leave the van, but she didn't want to go.

"Ricardo!" She whined. "I brought you here and I deserve to know what you tell them."

"No, you don't, Nancy," I said.

"Go on out and have a smoke," Rick said.

"I don't want a fucking cigarette," Nancy pouted.

Ricardo looked at her and said, "Hey, no hard feelings, baby, but you talk a lot. I don't want no one knowing what I say!"

Nancy took some convincing, but she finally stepped out and lit up, sipping on the last beer.

"Nancy doesn't know anything, man," Ricardo said. "But, she talks too much and the cops listen to her. Nancy's a snitch and we all know it, but we let her hang out 'cause she's cute – basically harmless."

"She's fucking cute all right," I said and Rick nodded with his eyes wide open.

"You gotta promise, man. Don't tell Nancy anything I tell you guys. I know you're trying to solve the murders, but I'm not getting killed because of her big mouth."

"Fair enough," Rick said.

"It was around the time those girls were missing from Yosemite," Ricardo said.

"Do you remember the month?" I asked.

"I think it was February, the middle of February," Ricardo said. "Mick was working on my car, and I was just hanging out. I was here for a couple of hours and I had a few beers in me, so I needed to take a piss. Mick told me to go into the garage and piss. There were people in the neighborhood walking around. I opened the garage doors and walked in and that's when I saw the girl."

"What girl?" Rick said.

"You saw a girl?" I said.

"Fucking-A, I did," Ricardo said. "I didn't know who she was, never saw her before."

"How old was the girl?" I said.

"Around sixteen or seventeen," Ricardo said. "She was sitting, hunkered down on the dirt in the back corner of the garage."

Rick and I stared at each other. Holy shit! I couldn't believe what we'd just heard. I asked Ricardo if he told the FBI about the young girl.

"Of course I did. They showed me photographs of the missing mother and daughter, and that girl from South America. I didn't recognize any of them as the one I saw in Mick's garage."

"Was it dark inside?" Rick said. "Did you get a good look at her?"

"I could see fine," Ricardo said.

"Ricardo," I said, "is it at all possible that the girl in Mick's garage was Juli Sund?

"No." Ricardo said.

"If that wasn't Juli Sund in the garage," I said, "who was it?"

"Some girl, I don't fucking know," Ricardo said. "Mick always has young doped-up girls around."

"So, seeing the girl in the garage wasn't a newsflash?" I said.

"You got to know Mick, man," Ricardo said. "He likes young chicks. He's a fucking deviant, a sick pervert. He always has young girls around, just like his brother. Mick likes to beat them before fucking them. It's his foreplay when he's loaded on the shit. He shoots them up with dope, and if they don't do what he wants, they get beat and then, he fucks 'em."

"What about Dykes?" I said.

"What about him?" Ricardo said.

"Was Dykes around when you saw the girl?" I said.

"The day after I saw the girl in Mick's garage, I ran into Gene. He said he was in the mountains camping in the snow."

"Camping in the snow," I repeated. "Where?"

"Some place up by Mariposa," Ricardo said.

The girl in Michael Larwick's garage was surprising news and very bothersome. Rick and I both agreed it might have been Juli, but the fact that Eugene Dykes had been "camping in the snow" somewhere up in Mariposa was really troubling.

Ricardo wasn't telling us everything he knew; guys like him never do. But the timing of the abductions, the young girl in Larwick's garage, Larwick's former residence in Long Barn, along with Dykes trip to Mariposa painted a nasty picture for the Yosemite murders.

I felt like it was coming together.

For all her imperfections, Nancy had done well.

CHAPTER 38

May 2002
Sacramento, California

"WE FINALLY TALK"

AT THE END of May 2002, I contacted agent, Val Sankin of the California Department of Justice, Bureau of Investigation. I'd met Agent Sankin a few years back through a good friend who was also with DOJ. Agent Sankin had been the lead investigator for DOJ on the Yosemite murders.

I was ready to bring my entire investigation to the table, to anyone who would listen. Everything was smoke and mirrors with law enforcement, and the closer I felt that I was getting to the truth, the harder it was to get anyone to listen.

I was past being frustrated; I was burning out.

"I need to know who's on board with us, Val," I said. "I keep hitting walls each time I talk to anybody."

"Besides myself and Camps, I have no idea who to go to. You knew you were on your own." He paused. "Frankly Steve, I think you've handled yourself pretty well. You know we had to keep you at arm's length. That came down from the top. As far as anybody knows, we've got the bad guy."

"Yeah," I said. "But what about the other bad guys? What about the victims' families? Don't they deserve to know the truth?"

Sankin sighed, but then, he gave in. "O.K., Sanzeri. I'll take your report, for now, but I have no idea who will accept it. We all understand that a 'can of worms' is not what prosecutors want to open up at this point."

Yeah, I got it. The "can of worms" he was talking about were the scumbags who'd played dirty with Stayner. With that guy as a slam-dunk, who'd want to bring in complications like Candler, Larwick, and Dykes? The public's taste for blood had been satisfied; why rock the boat?

But, Agent Sankin had read the report and found it interesting.

So, he decided to walk it up. He headed for the California State Attorney General's Office and met with Agent Nick Canozeri. Agent Canozeri had been the lead investigator representing the Attorney General's office on the Yosemite case. He was also on the prosecution team with Mariposa and the FBI. I reminded Agent Sankin about Calaveras County District Attorney, Peter Smith and how (Smith) failed to send my report to Canozeri, two years earlier.

"Maybe it will be different this time," Agent Sankin said.

I wasn't holding my breath, but I knew Sankin would do his best. Two days later he called.

"It's early," Agent Sankin said. "Sorry if I woke you."

"No, I'm up" I said. "What's going on?"

"Nick Canozeri called yesterday."

"Oh yeah, what did he say?"

"Are you ready for this?"

"Hit me," I said.

"Canozeri didn't want the reports. He wouldn't even take the copies. I was stunned to hell and back."

I was speechless and could not believe it.

"You have got to be fucking kidding," I said. "Tell me you are."

"Seriously," Agent Sankin said. "Canozeri told me that he would have to investigate your statements before accepting the information as evidence and that it was too late for that."

"Can he do this?" I said.

"To a certain degree he can, but eventually, if you push it, they will have to accept what you have. We just need to get to the right person."

"Anyone in mind?" I said.

"I think it's time for the FBI," Agent Sankin said. "Nick Rossi is the guy we want."

"What's the difference, Val? Nick Rossi is heading the prosecution team. He knows what's been happening. Rossi is well aware of me, has been for a while."

Val told me that he trusted Nick Rossi. Apparently, they knew each other pretty well. He also explained that the Feds had a different agenda with the case. They also had more power. It was a government thing, and this time I should expect a response.

FBI Special Agent Nick Rossi was the spokesperson for the FBI's Sacramento office. He'd been involved with the Yosemite case since the beginning, and he'd replaced Agent Jeff Rinek, who had led the investigation from the beginning.

It had been a strange move by FBI Special Agent in Charge, James Maddock. Jeff Rinek was the field agent in charge of the case, and he liked Eugene Dykes as a suspect. Then, poof! Rinek was taken off the case and reassigned.

But, now Nick Rossi was the Special Agent in Charge of the Sacramento office. He replaced James Maddock, who, along with two other agents, were demoted and reassigned elsewhere, early on in the case. Maddock lost his "stripes" due to the way he handled the investigation, and more.

I had something in common with Agent Nick Rossi. We'd graced the same newspaper pages when Paul Candler was arrested in Alabama. I was anxious to see how Agent Rossi would react to me now.

Friday morning, May 7, arrived cloudy and wet. I was outside cleaning up trash from a dog or a raccoon's early morning visit, and it was a mess. My pager sounded and it displayed, "Private Number." Then the phone rang.

"I wanted to see if there's anything you need or have questions about," Rossi said. "I spoke with Val Sankin and he said you wanted to talk. If you needed any help or have something we can work with I'd like to know about it. I saw the newspaper stories and thought you would like to talk."

"Thanks," I said. "I appreciate that. I have been trying to talk to someone for a long time, Agent Rossi. I sent reports to the task force two years ago. Did you ever read them?"

"I did, but there wasn't much to go on."

"You're right," I said, "it was a little light, but not now."

"I take it that your investigation has expanded," Agent Rossi said.

"Very much so," I said. "I've had pertinent information for a long time, including new information from witnesses you subpoenaed to the Grand Jury."

"What can we do with your investigation?" Rossi said.

"Morrissey is going to bring in other suspects you named earlier. She will present a reasonable doubt defense and this will lessen your chances for a conviction on Stayner. I know you don't want this."

"That's right, I don't. So?" Rossi said.

"I have more on Larwick, Dykes, and Candler. I'm certain that Morrissey will be subpoenaing one or all of them. When that time comes you'll need what I have."

"Sanzeri, you went to the *Modesto Bee* with a lot of this shit. You could have phoned me first."

"Only once, on September 30th. The *Bee* ran the other stories without my knowing. I figured you would have contacted me after the first story broke."

"Well, you might have figured out that I was kind of busy after the eleventh of September."

"I'm sorry Agent Rossi," I said. "I think the whole country was pretty distracted around that time."

"Call me Nick," Rossi said. "So what have you got since?"

Agent Rossi got an ear full. I was selective with names and places, but told him enough to keep his interest.

"O.K. That's fine," Agent Rossi said, "But getting your witnesses to stick to their stories in front of a Grand Jury is what counts."

"I agree, dopers change their stories all the time, but I have video and audio taped interviews and that's hard to dispute. And I think I can get a witness to come forward."

"Thinking you can do something and actually doing it are two distinctly different things, Steve."

"Next to my loyalty to the Carringtons and to the case, I have an allegiance to my informants. They know I won't burn them. Witness protection needs to be in the cards."

"Fair enough," Rossi said. "So, what do you need from me?

"Nothing at this time, but I had some questions."

"Sure, ask away," Agent Rossi said.

"Why didn't you like Paul Candler?"

"I saw no connection between Candler and the murders. There's just no physical evidence against Paul Candler, nor is there any connection to Cary Stayner."

"You sure about that?" I said. "I can put Candler with Stayner at the Cedar Lodge. Look at his residence in Moccasin, his flight to Alabama, his criminal history, and the statements he and Barbara Dobbins made to me and Rick?"

"Compelling and circumstantial is all you have. Are you sure

156

you just don't have allegations?"

"Candler incriminated himself to my partner Rick. Candler ran to Alabama to hide from you guys. Candler wasn't running on my bond."

"Candler was just paranoid," Agent Rossi said.

"No, it was more than that," I said. "What about the statewide manhunt? Every cop in Alabama had a copy of the wanted poster, but your Agent Barnes demanded that I stop."

"We only wanted to question Candler, that was it."

"Rick and I would be glad to take a polygraph."

"That may not be necessary," Agent Rossi said.

"All of the suspects you named in the investigation never left the valley or the Mother Lode, let alone run away as far as Alabama."

"It was the wanted poster," Agent Rossi said. "Candler must have seen one of them and left California."

"I don't think so," I said. "He was gone from California by the time I printed the posters."

"Then, I have no idea why he'd go that far."

We left it at that for the moment. I thought my phone call with Agent Rossi had gone pretty well. He didn't tell me everything, but I didn't tell him everything either. Rossi was going to meet with fellow prosecutors and said he'd call me back later.

At ten of six in the evening, Agent Rossi phoned back.

"Marcia Morrissey announced that she's bringing in the other scumbags," I said. "Most people still believe Cary Stayner did not act alone."

"I saw the paper, Steve," Agent Rossi said. "Let them believe what they want. We had physical evidence on Stayner and there was none on anyone else. The map he sent took us right to Juli Sund's body."

"What about the pink blanket fibers found in Dykes' Jeep Cherokee?" I said.

"It proves very little," Agent Rossi said. "There are millions of pink blankets out there. They're in hotel and motel rooms all over."

"Fiber evidence is usually good stuff."

"Not in this case," Agent Rossi said, "just too common."

"Didn't the blanket fibers on Juli, match the fibers found on Dykes' jacket and in his jeep?"

"Our lab said they were similar," Agent Rossi said, "but not an exact match."

I switched gears. "I always wondered how Stayner could get three women to cooperate so easily," I said. "Carole would have fought for Juli and Silvina. The only way Stayner would've been able to pull off the kidnapping alone would be if he had a gun."

"Stayner had a gun," Rossi said.

This was news to me. I had most of the major details, but no one had ever said anything about a firearm. Francis Carrington never mentioned a gun.

"You're telling me that Cary Stayner had a gun," I said. "He used a pistol, an automatic. We have it booked into evidence."

I still didn't like it. It's hard to tie someone up with one hand while holding a gun in the other. I didn't ask how Stayner pulled it off, and I decided to leave it alone for the moment.

Agent Rossi said he would be in touch.

CHAPTER 39

June 2002
San Jose, California

"WITNESS & CYBER SLEUTH"

PRIOR TO STAYNER'S trial, there were several closed court hearings. Marcia Morrissey challenged her client's confession to the FBI. She believed that the FBI had coerced Stayner into saying he killed the victims without help. Morrissey presented the motion to dismiss the confession and Judge Hastings denied it.

Cary Stayner's trial on July 15, 2002, was just around the corner. It was now mid-June, and 648 citizens arrived at Santa Clara County Superior Court as potential jurors. The press was at full speed with journalists, cameramen, producers, and support staff flooding the courthouse grounds. It was becoming a sideshow.

Newspapers printed daily accounts of the day's activities. As for Rick and me, things were quiet. My most recent contact with Nick Rossi was on June 3, and he was only checking in. I had nothing new and the FBI wasn't fishing. The valley was dead, and Nancy Lawson was out of touch.

The Stayner defense plowed ahead as planned. My cue would come when Dykes, Larwick, or Candler took the witness stand. That's what I wanted, and I was crossing my fingers.

It was July 5, and the jury pool had been whittled down to 12 jurors plus four alternates. Selection went smoothly, with very little argument over dismissals from either side.

Then, the following day, Marcia Morrissey shocked everybody with a post court press conference. I couldn't believe it. Nine days until Stayner's trial, and she suddenly decides that an "insanity" defense would be more appropriate.

The air left my sails. Was Morrissey an idiot? There was no way in hell that Cary Stayner would beat his case with an insanity defense. He wasn't found insane when he killed Joie Armstrong, and she was murdered after Carole, Juli and Silvina. Why this move by

Morrissey and so late in the game?

She was making a big mistake and Stayner didn't have a chance. She had to know this. Morrissey was throwing in the towel and this was what Rossi and the prosecution wanted.

Keep the other dirt-bags out of the courtroom, and there would be no reasonable doubt.

The prosecution was going for the death penalty all the way. Capital punishment expert, George Williamson was retained by the prosecution for that purpose. If Cary Stayner was found insane, he would avoid the gas chamber. If he was convicted and not insane, the death penalty could be handed down.

It was never a question of Cary Stayner's involvement with the kidnapping and murders of Carole, Juli and Silvina. The court of public opinion supported this and a respectable number already bet the farm that he was guilty along with some other scumbags.

When the 35 page questionnaire was handed to the final 62 prospective jurors, 48 percent believed Cary Stayner was guilty. Pleading guilty to Joie's death had sealed Stayner's fate with California's case. The prejudice was overwhelming. It was obviously a dead end for Stayner, and Morrissey believed she could only save her client's life by saying he was nuts.

July 15, 2002, and the trial of Cary Anthony Stayner began. Opening arguments went well for both sides. No cameras were allowed in the courtroom, but news was timely each evening.

Two days into the Stayner trial and I was pleasantly surprised when Rhonda Dunn from Chicago phoned from the San Francisco airport. She had five days' vacation and had decided to visit her uncle in Redwood City, 23 miles north of Santa Clara County Superior Court. A few months earlier, Rhonda had mentioned something about taking a shot at getting into the courtroom.

After two days in San Jose and a football field distance from the courthouse, Rhonda phoned and said she was on her way to my place. She arrived that evening around 9:40.

"You made it!" I said, welcoming her. "Here, let me help you with your bags."

"Thanks, there's one more in the back seat," she said.

"I really wasn't sure you were coming out west," I said.

"I told you I was," she said. "We talked about it."

"Well, you made it. I'm glad to see you. Come on in."

160

Rhonda followed behind as I carried two large suit cases, a purple duffle bag, and an oversized black leather purse, upstairs to the guest bedroom.

"Lots of luggage for five days," I said.

"Maybe longer, who knows," Rhonda said, giving me the sugar pie eye.

"What are you drinking?" I asked as I dropped the luggage.

"If you have wine, red would be nice."

A year had passed since we met for the first time at the Hyatt Hotel in Burlingame. Mike Mooney met with the both of us, on the *Modesto Bee's* dime. It was an interview situation. Rhonda and I spent the evening together and I got to know how she ticked.

Rhonda was wearing the same white hip-huggers and looked just as good. She was nicely tanned and her hair was lighter and longer. I poured two glasses of cabernet and showed her around.

"Let's sit out on the deck," I said. "More wine?"

"A little breezy out here; I don't feel like getting my sweater."

"Fine by me," I said. "Let's hangout inside."

"You have some pictures of Paul Candler I haven't seen."

I'd hoped to stay away from the case that evening and relax in front of the television or listen to the stereo. But, she wanted to get at it right away. She came out to California with specific intentions of working on the case. I was discovering that Rhonda Dunn was a cyber-sleuth.

"I'll show you in the morning," I said, "let's kick it. You've had a long trip."

"I'm fine," Rhonda said. "Let's look at the photos. Come on, bring the bottle."

I led her to the living room and put on some Tony Bennett. I opened Candler's file, removing several photographs. He was shirtless in three of them. Rhonda sat across from me and looked at each one closely.

"I remember this freak like it was yesterday," she said. "See, that's the devil tattoo I told Mooney about. I recognize most of the tattoos on his arms. He was close to me."

"What else do you notice about him?" I said. "See anything new that jumps out at you?"

"He was wearing the same black T-shirt and levis," she said.

"Look, see his monkey legs?"

"Bowlegged? You're so right," I said. "He walks like an ape that's for sure."

Rhonda sat back on the couch and sipped her wine.

"Take a look at these for me," I said. "Do you recognize any of them, Rhonda?"

"The FBI already showed me these perverts . . . same photos. If they were with Candler and Stayner, I would have said so. Paul Candler is the only one I recognized with Cary Stayner. You know that I never saw Candler in the newspaper."

Rhonda filled her glass and then mine.

"I know that," I said. "His photo only ran once in the Sonora paper."

"I'm really tired," she said. "I'm ready for bed."

I never doubted what Rhonda saw at the Cedar Lodge, just that she came off like an airhead at times, but she was smart and articulate, and there was one thing about this respiratory therapist that the FBI overlooked or ignored: Rhonda Dunn had a photographic memory.

I had one more photo to show her before bedtime.

"I'm a little tired, too, but just take a look at this last one," I said.

"What!" She shrieked and jumped to her feet. "I don't believe this! Oh my God!" She began to tremble. I pulled her back down to the sofa.

"Hey, take it easy, Rhonda. What the fuck is it?" I asked.

"Oh my God, he was with Candler, and Stayner. This was the other guy who followed me around the parking lot."

I was holding a photograph of Eugene Dykes from a very early story in the *Sacramento Bee* dated March 24, 1999. This was the Stanislaus County Jail booking photo that was taken after Dykes' arrest. In this picture, he had long hair and a goatee.

A week later, Dykes' latest booking photo from state prison was released to the press, but it showed Dykes with a shaved head and no facial hair. He looked like two different people.

Rhonda was pale. "This is the other guy that was stalking my mother and me. Oh my God." She took a gulp of wine. "Who is he?"

At this point, I wanted to be sure she was accurate.

"Are you sure he's one of the idiots you saw?" I asked.

She looked at me. "Steve, you know I have a photographic

memory. I'm positive. Who is he? I've never seen this photo!"

I moved the two photographs of Eugene Dykes side by side. At first, Rhonda was confused and then, she got it. "He just shaved his beard and hair off. Oh my God. It's the same guy!"

I got that same old adrenaline surge since this case had grabbed hold of me from the beginning.

Rhonda had just put Eugene Dykes with Stayner and Candler at the Cedar Lodge. The FBI's first target was now identified by the most valuable eyewitness to the case.

And if the FBI discounted Rhonda, how come they drug her into their Chicago headquarters just prior to charging Cary Stayner in the state's case?

Rhonda ended up staying with me for two days, two days that were good for both of us, and then she left for home. I reminded her to keep it hushed, even more so than in the past. I told her not to call me until I'd made my move.

I didn't need to remind her about the Fed's raid at her place.

"Wire taps are alive and well," I explained to Ms. Dunn more than once.

CHAPTER 40

July 2002
Murphys, California

"MOVES EVERYWHERE"

THE STAYNER TRIAL was ending its second week, and jurors were already tired of listening to repeated testimonies of psychiatrists. Five in all, each one stated that Cary Stayner was crazy. Past trauma and the kidnapping of Stayner's brother, Steven, were to blame for Stayner's savage actions. After nine days the defense rested.

Although the prosecuting agency was Mariposa County, Agent Rossi was calling the shots. The FBI had the resources and manpower. They led the Joie Armstrong murder investigation. Rossi and Co. already pinned one murder on Stayner, so the State's case should be a slam-dunk. As long as reasonable doubt didn't enter the courtroom, the prosecution would win. The prosecution opened and finished presenting their case in eight days. This trial was moving fast.

Fourth week into the trial and Ms. Morrissey was at it again. "More Doctors for The Defense?" the *San Jose Mercury* headlined on Monday. It was obvious the defense was losing and Morrissey needed to buy some time and figure out how to strengthen her client's case. When it's all said and done, the outcome would either be: Cary Stayner is guilty by reason of insanity or not guilty by reason of insanity, but found sane and guilty. My money was on the prosecution.

The Yosemite murder investigation never lacked attention or scrutiny from the media. From the start, this wasn't an easy investigation, but it could have been handled better. Too many dismissals of viable witnesses and suspects had backfired on investigators.

This was never truer after heads rolled and asses were chewed, and high ranking FBI personnel were handed transfers out of Sacramento, including Special Agent in Charge, James Maddox.

Saturday July 24, and NBC aired a one hour *Dateline* special about the "Yosemite Sightseer Murders," and the timing couldn't have been better or worse, depending who you were rooting for.

I was hoping to pick-up some new information but instead found myself choked up. This case was very personal to me. *Dateline's* photos of Carole with Juli, when Juli was a baby girl, hit me hard, a young mother with her two-year-old daughter. Now they were gone forever.

And then there was Silvina; what a beautiful young woman. She came to this great country alive, vibrant and happy, and left in a coffin, never to see America again. And there's Joie. She accomplished her dreams through hard work, perseverance and a love of nature. She was living her dream until Stayner took her life.

Dateline was skeptical about Cary Stayner as the lone killer. Michael Larwick and Eugene Dykes images slid across the screen. Thousands of viewers rekindled their beliefs of multiple suspects. With Dykes and Larwick, front and center in living rooms across America, I wondered how much influence this would have over the trial.

On July 29, the shit hit the fan big time, and the *San Jose Mercury Newspaper* was the first to break the story. It was Marcia Morrissey's latest move; one she should have done all along.

Morrissey announced that she would introduce an FBI videotaped confession of Eugene "Rufus" Dykes, and, suddenly, the prosecution was scrambling. Rossi's team was thrown a wicked curve. For the first time, reasonable doubt would be presented at trial.

This was what I wanted and what Nick Rossi feared. Hell, two scumbags confessed and only one was being held to answer. Stayner and Dykes' confessions had holes and inaccuracies, but also supported matching statements and information only the killers could possibly have known.

I never understood why Morrissey went with the insanity defense in the first place. Stayner had a good shot in the State's case because other suspects were named. Morrissey was planning to divert the responsibility from Cary Stayner to Eugene Dykes, and it was not too late to try. The prosecution was going to have to retrace their tracks.

Timing is everything and now it felt like it was my time. But, like everything in this case, it all went to hell in a hand basket.

Before lunch, the following day, Judge Hastings denied Morrissey's motion and the tape was scratched from the prospective evidence list. Judge Hastings based his decision on the fact that Stayner's insanity plea did not allow for reasonable doubt and that the tape would present just that.

The prosecution argued and won that battle. But, before Agent Rossi could relax, another bomb landed. Top news story the next day, *"Eugene Dykes Subpoenaed In Stayner Murder Trial."* I called my partner.

"It looks as though it's working out the way I'd hoped," I said. "Did you see the *Bee?*"

"Yeah, I caught it this morning," Rick said. "Take a look at the news on Channel 13. They just mentioned Eugene Dykes. So, are you ready for this volcano to erupt?"

"Sure as shit I am," I said. "This is what we've been working for, for three years. It's the way it should have been all along."

"Do you trust Rossi?" Rick said.

"He's been good so far," I said.

"Are you giving him everything?"

"No, but Nick, will be cautious with what he asks for."

Rick laughed at that. "Nick? You guys buddies?"

"Sure, we are. I'm his new best friend."

CHAPTER 41

August 2002
Sacramento, California

"THE NEGOTIATION"

EIGHT THIRTY SATURDAY morning, August 8, and I wanted to talk with agent Rossi. The power of a subpoena is about as good as it gets, and it would be near impossible for Judge Hastings to stop the defense's subpoena of Eugene Dykes. Rossi had to be worried, and I had some ideas. I made the call and left a message. Ten minutes later the phone rang.

"My plan was to phone you later today," Agent Rossi said.

"I didn't want to wait until Monday," I said. "I'm not disturbing you, am I?"

"No, happy you phoned," Agent Rossi said. "I'll be in meetings all day anyway."

"With all that's going on, I thought we should talk."

"I certainly do," Agent Rossi said. "So, you understand about Eugene Dykes?"

"I do and it concerns me," I said.

"We're on the same page, good."

"We are. How do you want to handle this?"

"You have things to tell me regarding Eugene Dykes," Rossi said. "He will be appearing in court and this is a problem for our side."

"Off the record," I said.

"Sure," Agent Rossi said. "You know I am interested in your investigation, but I need to be selective. We do not want to screw up Stayner's trial."

"I understand your position, Nick, and I think I can help. If Dykes testifies or takes the fifth, his appearance alone could sway the jury. It could be a fucking mess."

"Well stated," Agent Rossi said, "you understand my dilemma."

"There's a way to handle it."

"Tell me," he said.

"I'll only turnover what I think you may need at the time you might need it. You don't know what I have and as far as you're concerned, I have nothing. The two investigation reports were early on and who knows what I came upon after 1999."

"O.K., I'm with you," Agent Rossi said. "You are not withholding information that may or may not exist, but it might exist if I need it."

"That's right," I said, "you can't get into trouble with your people, and I won't get indicted for withholding information."

"That's fine," Agent Rossi said, "but you only talk to me."

"I wouldn't have it any other way," I said.

"O.K., I've met with my people, and we've decided to take a close look at your investigation."

"Are your people on the same page as you and I?"

"They understand. We would want updated reports, tapes, statements, information that would help us if Eugene Dykes testifies. It's when I need the information, specifically."

"My investigation is the crutch. You just received information from the Carringtons' private investigator that very recently surfaced."

"I think that could work," Agent Rossi said.

"Nick, I'm the can opener for the worms. You just have to control the slimy guys."

"Not a problem. Just bring me something I can pin on Eugene Dykes before he takes the stand. And one more thing, you cannot tell anyone about our conversations including your partner, Rick Janes."

"Got it," I said.

CHAPTER 42

August 2002
San Jose, California

"NICE TRY"

ON AUGUST 12TH, Eugene "Rufus" Dykes, appeared in the Santa Clara County Superior Courthouse as a witness for the defense. After raising his right hand and being sworn in, Eugene Dykes sat in the witness chair and read from a piece of paper that his court appointed attorney wrote an hour earlier. "In fear of incriminating myself, I choose not to testify, and therefore I am exercising my Fifth Amendment Rights."

Everyone anticipated that Eugene Dykes would take the Fifth. No way in hell was he going to testify. But, that little one minute court appearance had to have sprinkled some reasonable doubt amongst members of the jury. Jurors were attentive from the time Eugene's name was called, and he shuffled in, until the sounds of leg irons faded away as he was escorted out. The prosecution could not measure how much jurors were influenced by Dykes visit.

"I need something as soon as you can get it," Agent Rossi said, during a phone conversation after court. "Dykes' appearance has opened that can of worms."

"Name it," I said.

"A report," Agent Rossi said. "Typed; a few paragraphs regarding your interview with Rick Stiles. What he said, and anything else you remember him telling you. Don't mention the recording in your report."

"I'll have it to you in an hour," I said.

"I'll be with the prosecution team tonight, at least until ten. I'd like to hand them something before we adjourn."

Agent Rossi, asking for an investigation report was a big deal to me. Finally, my work had paid off. Rossi received my two page report at 9:01 p.m.

I never heard back from him.

On August 26, 2002, Cary Stayner was found guilty in the murders of Carole Sund, Juli Sund and Silvina Pelosso.

On September 17, 2002, the jury found Cary Stayner, sane when he took the lives of the trio. All 12 jurors believed that Stayner knew exactly what he was doing when he kidnapped and murdered Carole, Juli and Silvina.

On December 12th, 2002, Cary Anthony Stayner was sentenced to death by lethal injection. San Quentin State Prison in California became his new residence and will remain as such until Mr. Stayner arrives in hell.

There were unanswered questions, lots of them. We'd handed them Paul Candler and nothing happened. I wanted Eugene Dykes to be exposed, and he was. I successfully negotiated my evidentiary position with the FBI, and it had worked. Short of dragging in an informant that would testify, our investigation went well.

Was I ready to turn the page and take a sneak peek at the next chapter? First, I needed to take a deep breath and decide if I wanted any more of this? But the case chose me. It was a calling.

Did the Carringtons', Sunds' or Pelossos' want me to continue the investigation? It would be very difficult and painful for the families to bear another trial or possibly two or three more trials. Francis and Carole Carrington remained convinced that Cary Stayner had help. Jens Sund felt the same. Even after Stayner was convicted for the triple homicide, the public continued to believe that multiple killers were the play.

Will the FBI or Mariposa ever go after Eugene "Rufus" Dykes, Michael "Mick" Larwick, and Paul Candler Jr.? Probably not, not without a huge push.

Another thing that has continued to haunt me ever since I saw Stayner's letter to the FBI telling them where to find Juli Sund's body.

He said: "We had our way with her."

"*We*?" Who the fuck was "we?"

CHAPTER 43

March 2003
Murphys, California

"NOT FORGOTTEN"

THREE MONTHS HAD passed since Stayner's trial ended. The press slowed its coverage to a halt, except for an occasional blurb about Cary's one-hour yard-time or the number of letters he was receiving from twisted female fanatics.

I had no interest hearing about how Stayner was getting along in San Quentin, but I paid attention. The media remained interested in Stayner for several reasons, but mainly because no one believed that he acted alone.

It was March 7, just after 7:00 in the evening, and a call came as I was starting my exercise routine. I ignored the phone and went to the back deck for the jump rope. Five minutes of rope work and then hills. I started jumping and the phone rang again. I let it go to the machine and finished my second set. A glass of water in hand, I checked the machine. It was my neighbor, Jim. I returned his call.

"Where in 'Sam Houston' were you?" Jim said. "I've called twice. Your car's there."

"Yeah, I'm here, too." I said, "Just heading out the door. What's up?"

"Quick, Steve, turn to KOVR channel 13."

"What in the hell is so urgent?" I said.

"Something about the Yosemite murders," Jim said

For the most part, my neighbor was fairly up to date with the Yosemite Sightseer case. He lived across the street and liked to ask me questions about it. Retired, with not a hell of a lot to do, Jim watched television and drank plenty of beer.

"I got it on Jim, thanks and I'll talk to you later."

"Wait!" Jim said.

"What is it?"

"How about some company? Got a twelve-pack of suds on ice,

could be fun."

"Sure, maybe later."

I turned on the television and raised the volume. Channel 13 had my full attention. "*Did Cary Stayner act alone?*" as it was titled. The media was still asking.

The way I looked at it, "KOVR" put the Yosemite case back on the market, and there was no mistaking the message. This one-hour special really brought it to the surface. The fourth annual Carole Sund/Carrington Memorial Reward Foundation, "Vigil of Hope" was only three days away, and I planned on attending.

I arrived in downtown Modesto on Saturday afternoon. This would be the third time I'd participated in the walk and vigil for Carole, Juli and Silvina. Each year, more people joined the march, and each time I attended there were more photographs and flyers of murder victims and missing family members. It was overwhelming to see the booths and tables that were manned by loved-ones asking for help.

As I walked along gazing at sad and seemingly helpless folks, it felt as if I was at a Carnival of Death. People were reaching out to me for help. It was a very dark feeling. It was like a bad nightmare. And even sadder, this year was also a vigil of prayer for Lacy and Conner Peterson, two more brutal murders that shocked a nation.

I spent a few minutes with Francis and Carole Carrington, until they got scooped up by reporters and on camera interviews. I refrained from discussing any business and cut my visit short. We'd catch up later.

I helped myself to the free hotdogs and drinks, and meandered around the large gathering that filled the park. I looked for familiar faces and saw a few. Some were cops and investigators from the case. I saw a few local dopers I was familiar with, and there were two former bail clients. As the vigil came to a close, I met with the Carringtons, who introduced me to the Levy's. Francis Carrington led me past the stage and to Chandra's parents.

"Steve is our family investigator," Francis said.

"Nice to meet you," I said, as I greeted the Levy's.

"Francis told us a lot about you," Mr. Levy said. "If you think you can help us is any way, we'd be grateful."

"I'd be glad to help in any way I can," I said.

172

I agreed to look into Chandra's death, but it wouldn't be easy. I have to admit, I wasn't ready to jump into another huge case. I had become a go-to-guy and investigator, but there was only so much death I could take.

Especially when bad guys got away with murder.

CHAPTER 44

June – January 2003
San Diego, California

"CAN'T GET AWAY FROM THE CASE"

IT WAS EARLY June when I began losing interest in my work. I was burned-out. What began four years earlier as a simple bounty hunt had turned into a murder investigation that took a lot out of me. I needed a break and San Diego was the answer. I liked it down there. It was a big city with plenty of work, and I had friends.

I landed in beautiful San Diego, California, mid July of 2003. I shacked-up with longtime friend, Mimi Baker, a TV and movie script supervisor. I bummed around for a few weeks, splitting time with Mimi on the set, and hanging out at Mission beach. The days of sun and waves, followed by warm breezy evenings and margaritas alongside tanned babes on the beach, was just what the doctor ordered.

I quickly understood why people check out for this lifestyle. It was fucking great, so long as money was an easy commodity. No one really knew me or what I was about. But, now I was developing a huge bar tab. So, after an accelerated highlife and a diminishing bank account, I started to pursue employment.

A man's reputation is all he has when it comes down to it, and mine was well known in the bail bond and bounty hunting world. I had no goods for sale, just me. All I had to do was make a call, and I was in. My reputation was a step ahead. With the exception of Dan Cuellar of Fresno, Bob Burton of Tombstone, Stan Rifkin of New York, Ray Hawkins from Los Angeles, and Lance Wilkerson (RIP) out of Connecticut, I was probably the next most familiar bounty hunter in the industry.

There have never been a lot of us and it only takes a few cases with some "hair," and you soon become a reputable bail enforcement agent.

So, I needed a job, and the quickest most sensible idea would be to bounty hunt. I wasn't that thrilled about chasing fugitives into the hours. I was looking for a change, but I didn't have a lot of options.

I asked legendary bail bondsman, George "King" Stahlman (RIP) for a job. The "King" was the bail King and he owned the biggest bail agency in San Diego County. No way was I pussyfooting around with any other agencies.

George "King" Stahlman was a WWll Flying "Ace," and got into bail bonding after the war. The "King" owned the oldest agency in the state, and carried a bail license in good standing since 1946. After a short interview, I was hired. I was truly honored.

The "King" told me he liked my style. The "King" had skips, more than I had ever seen. Be careful what you wish for, as they say. My caseload was huge; more bail forfeitures than I had ever seen in one shot. Within a week, I was handed nine bounties, and there were more on the way.

My guess, King Stahlman Bail Bonding Company probably wrote at least 10 million dollars in bonds each year. With that kind of volume, there will be skips.

I chased bail jumpers from Solano Beach to the Mexican border, and I was actually having fun. New cities, new acquaintances - it was an adventure.

I mostly worked the investigations alone, until I was ready for a capture. Then I would drag along a few guys from the office. Sometimes I would have Bill Papenhausen, a retired San Diego cop and local PI, help me with a bounty. I also did some investigations for Bill, but that was short lived due to how little he paid. I liked Bill, but ten bucks an hour wasn't cutting it.

On a few occasions, I had met Papenhausen's former partner in the PI business; retired San Diego Police Sergeant, Manny Lopez.

Manny had his own PI firm and he was one of the best in San Diego County. Also, Manny was one of the main characters in Joseph Wambaugh's book, *"Lines and Shadows."* I read the book and can say that Manny was the man. He got into three "run n' guns," (shootouts) according to the nonfiction book.

The third week of August, and Bill Papenhausen had caught a homicide defense investigation and wanted me to work it. I had already quit, but Bill really needed me. He also asked Manny Lopez to help out, and that's when I said yes. It was a good opportunity to see a pro at work.

I did the crime scene sketch and Manny was impressed. A week later, I was working for "*Manny Lopez Investigations.*"

Manny paid me well, about $35.00 an hour, and I was flattered to be one of his only two investigators. There were plenty of retired cops in the area that would kill to work for Manny. I was seriously thinking of getting out of the bounty business, but Manny was keeping me busy and the hours were much better.

January 13, 2004, and the city of San Diego was blanketed with frost. This was my second winter here and it was much colder than the last. The sun was bright and pushing the 38 degree temperature up one digit at a time. I planned on setting out fairly early, but it was too cold and a little early, 6:35 a.m. Coffee and hot cocoa were my breakfast, along with a toke.

Hell, I wasn't going anywhere for a while, and it was Saturday. I had a bunch of boring reports to write and a court motion to-boot. I popped some "James Taylor" into the player and tried to decide which of the six reports I wanted to start.

I had quit the "King," last October and was now fulltime with Manny. A call came in and I grabbed it on the first ring. Damn early for a call, "hello!"

"I've been trying to find you for a fucking year, Steve," the caller said.

"Yeah, who the fuck is this?" I asked. "Jesus Christ it's a little early for a mouth like yours."

"I'm sorry," The caller said. "Where have you been?"

"Who is this?" I said.

"It's Nancy."

"Nancy," I said, "Nancy who?"

"Nancy Lawson, you ass. What, you fucking forgot about me?"

Memories of the Yosemite case swamped my mind. "Wow," I said, "what's going on?"

"Where have you been?" Nancy said.

"I'm down south."

"I've been trying to find you for a fucking month."

"I'm hiding. What do you want?"

"You won't believe what's happened," Nancy said. "I wish you were around. I need you to talk to someone. He knows everything about what happened to the girls. You need to get up here."

"Could be a little tough," I said. "The case is cold. So what's the urgency?"

"Oh, I see how it is," Nancy said, "you just don't fuck'n care anymore."

"Care about what?"

"Carole and Juli," Nancy said, "and Silvina . . . you've forgotten all about them."

I felt a stab somewhere in the middle of my chest, and then, I started getting steamed. "Bullshit. Of course, I care, Nancy. But it's over. Unlike you, I've moved on. Keep dwelling on this and it will kill you. Unless you have a big fish, my tackle is put away. Do you have a big fish for me, Nancy?"

"The biggest," Nancy said. "Get up here and talk to this guy. He wants to talk to you."

"And tell me what," I said. "What news will your friend have? Will he testify against Dykes or Larwick?"

"You know I can't say over the phone."

"Give me a hint," I said, "something to make me feel better."

"Um, he knows things."

"Things?" I asked, "What kind of things?"

She paused, and I could feel her trying to figure out how to say it. "He knows where things are buried," Nancy said. "You need to meet with him soon as possible. Please, I'm telling you this guy knows stuff that nobody else does."

God, I'd been chasing ghosts and rumors for so long, it was tough to get a hard on for this. "Listen Nancy, I am eight hours away. It's not that easy."

"One day to get up here. You should leave today."

Nancy was pushier than she'd ever been before. It had been over a year since we spoke and even longer since I'd seen her face-to-face.

"How's the beer habit?" I asked.

"Hardly there, but that's not what we're talking about. You need to get your ass up here, now!"

The longer I stayed on the line, the more I became convinced that I might have to check out what she was talking about. I started thinking if I had any business in Modesto, any bad guys to chase up north.

"I'll tell ya what," I said, "let me sleep on it."

"Sleep on what Steve, just do it."

I felt that old familiar tingle that always got me when I sensed something might be breaking. I felt that Nancy had something. I left my "Normal Heights" neighborhood at 8:30 Sunday morning, for "meth central." I hadn't done a thing on the Yosemite case for some time and I only hoped that Nancy's buddy wouldn't be full of shit.

I arrived in Modesto around dinnertime and checked into a motel off Highway 99 and Briggsmore. I headed over to the Chinese buffet across the street for some chow.

The plan was that I'd meet Nancy and "the guy" at around noon tomorrow. We'd worked it out that Nancy was going to act surprised to see me.

We spoke before bed and everything was in order. Several times, I had to assure Nancy that I would be there. She had been drinking.

"You better be sober tomorrow," I said.

"Fuck you," Nancy said, "don't worry about me."

I hit the sack with questions on my mind. What was I in for? I didn't know the guy's name or what he was going to blab about. Nancy wouldn't tell me over the phone, but that was the way we did it.

I'd trained her pretty good.

CHAPTER 45

January 15, 2004
Modesto, California

"DAMN TWEAKERS"

I ARRIVED AT the mall at 11:57 a.m. and rang Nancy's cell.

"Steve, we're almost done eating and then he needs pants."

"What?" I said.

"Let me take Devin to get some pants," Nancy said. "I'll call you back in a few."

"I don't fucking believe this," I said. "Get the pants later."

I wasn't in the mood for fucking around. Every doper I have ever met wastes everybody's time.

"Steve, if you want this to work you have to let me do my thing. I need to meet you in front of Penny's. That's where the pants he likes are at."

"Half-hour and that's it," I said.

"I Promise!"

I drove around to the other side of the mall and parked. Half an hour was it and not a second later. I would drag Devin out of the dressing room if I had to. Quarter to one, and Nancy called, "We're heading out."

"Great, see ya in a minute," I said.

I hightailed it to Penny's, away from the front doors and sat on the bench in front. I then heard her voice.

"Steve, oh my God, how are, you?" Nancy said, very convincingly.

I stood and reached for Nancy, which wasn't difficult because she looked hotter than ever.

"Nancy, you look great!" I said, playing along.

We hugged each other and exchanged a kiss. Nancy felt good. I peeked at Devin, who was just behind Nancy. He wasn't enjoying the show.

"Steve, this is Devin, my friend," Nancy said. "Devin and I just had lunch and are shopping. What are you doing here?"

"Same thing," I said. "Hello Devin, nice to meet you."

Devin reached his hand out, and we made eye contact.

"Same here," Devin said.

"Devin is from down your way, Steve," Nancy said, "around the San Jose area."

"Alright," I said. "What do you do for dough?"

"Logging," Devin said.

"Is that right?" I said, "You a skidder?"

"Faller," Devin said.

Devin wasn't sure about me, but his eyes were curious. Obviously hot for Nancy, he appeared threatened with my presence and sat very close to her as they shared a smoke. Devin presented himself as a model doper, tweaker, and skinhead type. His sweatshirt couldn't cover all the sores on his hands, neck, and face, along with a pale skin tone covered by lots of tattoos.

Minus the attitude, Devin didn't seem too bad. He just had a bad meth habit; the norm in this area. He then noticed the "Hells Angels" support shirt I wore beneath my half buttoned over-shirt.

"You ride?" Devin said.

"That's right," I said. "Why do you ask?"

"The H.A. shirt," Devin said, "It's '81, right?"

"Sure is," I said. "Do you know any of the boys?"

"Maybe," Devin said, "but I don't know you."

"Fair enough," I said.

I went light on Devin and allowed him to get on top of me a little, so to speak. He needed to flex his muscles for his new squeeze. Nancy kept quiet and hardly intervened. Devin had no clue of the setup and relaxed a bit more as we spoke. It was going well, until Devin asked to leave with some excuse about picking his mother up from work.

I looked at Nancy, and she opened her arms for a hug. I then reached my hand out and Devin shook it more firmly than prior. He didn't say a word and released my hand as he turned away to grasp Nancy's hand.

As I stood and watched the pair stroll away, Nancy turned one last time. My hand simulated holding a phone and she nodded. Devin's mind was focused on his next high and maybe getting laid.

I got nothing that would help the case. I would call Nancy in a

180

few hours and ask her what the hell Devin was going to tell me. I wasn't a happy camper. But she beat me to it, and at 4:15 my hotel phone rang.

"You eating dinner?" Nancy said.

"No, what's up?" I said.

"He asked about you," Nancy said. "He said you kind of remind him of a narc."

"All the dopers think everyone's a cop," I said. "Other than that, what the fuck does he have to say?"

"He likes you and wants to meet you again," Nancy said. "He wants me to meet with him and show me the ditch where he buried the girls' clothes. I had to convince him you're not a cop, and I know he believes me."

"There's a ditch?" I said.

"The ditch on the ranch in Salida," Nancy said. "Devin worked as a ranch hand. Gene made Devin bury the girls' clothes in this ditch. It's the truth. He's taking me out there tonight."

"You knew about this," I said.

"Sure I did, I just couldn't tell you. Devin is having a hard time keeping this to himself. He will talk to you."

"You're going tonight," I said, "for sure?"

"He's picking me up at Safeway at eleven," Nancy said. "I'll call when I get back, I promise. And don't try to follow us."

Don't follow, are you nuts. I was just thinking of that as she finished. I might only get one shot. On the other hand, Nancy will take me there if there's really a ditch. I had to let her go. I think she was righteous on this one. I only needed Devin to be the same.

I anxiously waited to hear about Nancy's venture. I asked her to call when she got home, no matter the time. At 3:15 a.m., Nancy called and sounded tired.

"How'd it go?" I said.

"Oh, Steve, I did a rail, just a little. He wouldn't take me out there unless I did a line. I am so sorry."

"Hey, you did what you needed to do," I said. "Did you keep your pants on?"

"Barely," Nancy said. "Oh, no mistake, he wanted some. I took care of the other. Please don't judge me."

"Baby, you did fine. Did you see the ditch?"

181

"I did. Steve, I was scared. It was fucking creepy out there. It was so fucking dark."

I could tell she was upset.

"Are you alright?" I said.

"I'm fine," Nancy said.

"Tell me what happened?"

"He made me smoke some shit after we did a bump, and then I drove him out to the ranch. Steve, its way the fuck out there. Only one road goes in. It was dark. Devin took me to a hole, a ditch in the ground. We must have walked for ten minutes"

"How big was the ditch?" I said.

"I don't know, size of a big swimming pool. It's not a ditch, it's a hole."

"What did you see?" I said.

"He showed me some car parts," Nancy said.

"What else?" I said.

"A bag of women's clothes that was torn open," Nancy said.

"Women's clothes, you sure?"

"Steve, I was high, but I know what I saw. You need to fucking get to that ditch."

"Can you find it?"

"Sure," Nancy said. "I'll take you tonight."

We arrived at the ranch just before eleven, with only a sliver of the moon above. Nancy's directions were on target, but she refused to walk in with me. I parked under some walnut trees to hide my car.

"I can't do it again," Nancy said. "I got a bad feeling around that ditch. Got any weed?"

"I have a roach in my black bag. It's in the back. Stay here. You'll be fine."

"So, just follow that tree-line in," Nancy said. "You'll see an old windmill and it's just left of that on the path. Be careful."

I crept in slowly under the canopy of walnut trees and darkness. I was about 150 yards in, when I arrived at the windmill. The dusty path soon led me to a large hole in the ground. This was it, at least 50 feet across and a little longer. I saw the car parts, tires, wood pallets, metal drums, furniture and clothes. I stepped into the ditch for a closer look, and chills hit my spine as I picked up women's clothing.

I then moved around some car parts. They were from a late

182

1970's Jeep Cherokee, same model that Eugene Dykes was driving. Five years later, and I was looking at what might be the most important crime scene of the case.

I needed Devin.

CHAPTER 46

January 16, 2004
Modesto, California

"WITNESS PROTECTION IS IN THE CARDS"

IT WAS A sleepless night for me. I was onto something big. I was determined to move fast, but first I needed to capture Devin and get as much out of him as possible. I needed him to be my new best friend. I contacted Larry Murray, and told him my plan.

"Steve, listen to me," Larry said. "You need to watch yourself closely. Don't trust this guy, but use him. I got your back. Call me later."

Then, I called Nancy and she started the hunt for Devin. That afternoon she phoned.

"Steve, guess what?" Nancy said.

"Tell me," I said.

"Devin went in last night. He missed his drug class."

"Fuck! What's his bail amount?"

"Ten-thousand," Nancy said.

"Shit, O.K.," I said, "I'll take care of it. Let me make some calls."

"He needs out and you need him," Nancy said. And she was right. I was in a great position. I would be in control of Devin and he would have to talk to me. If I did him a favor, he would owe me one. I could also have his bond revoked if he decides to dick me around. I made some calls and had Devin, sprung.

Devin had no idea who posted his bail, so when I arrived as his chauffer, he was shocked to hell.

"Get in," I said.

"What the fuck is this?" Devin said.

"You're out of jail because of me. Get in the car."

Devin hesitated, but finally got in.

"So what the fuck is going on?" Devin said. "You a cop?"

"Nope, PI," I said.

"So, you are what Nancy told me," Devin said. "But brother, I

184

don't know if I can fucking trust you."

I know about the ranch in Salida," I said. "I saw the ditch."

"Fucking Nancy, God dammit" Devin said. "She has a big fucking mouth."

"She does," I said. "But you're here now, so let's talk."

"Hey, what the fuck," Devin said, "I didn't ask for this. Take me home."

"Devin, we can help each other," I said. "Tell me about the ditch."

"You saw it, nothing to tell."

"I saw it alright; caught my eye. Tell me, what do you know about the Yosemite murders?"

"I'm the fuck out of here!"

Devin reached for the door and I grabbed his arm.

"Get back here," I said. "I'm your new best friend right now. You have no one else. My guess is that this ditch holds evidence from the Yosemite murder case. Wouldn't you agree?"

Devin looked at me and I could see him give in. His eyes mellowed. I knew I hit a nerve.

"Devin, you're knee-deep in this shit and you want out," I said. "Your conscience is bothering you and I am the guy to talk to. There's a reason we're meeting together. I can get you witness protection."

Devin nodded slowly.

"How about lunch," I said.

"Sure," Devin said.

As I pulled into a Denny's parking lot, I couldn't help but think that this was it. I saw the ditch and now I had the gatekeeper.

"Thanks," I said, to the waitress as she completed our order. "Go on," I said, to Devin.

"You want to know about the Yosemite murders, I'll tell ya all I know. Just between me and you."

"You got it," I said.

"It was a Friday night and I stopped at David Montessa's house on the way to the store," Devin said. "He asked me to drop by to meet someone."

"Who?" I said

"He didn't say, but Gene would be there," Devin said.

"Dykes?"

"Yeah, why?"

"I wasn't aware that you knew Eugene Dykes," I said.

"Sure I do, he always has dope. Anyway, I pulled in front of David's house, out in Keys, and that's when I saw the red Pontiac and there were two girls in the back seat."

I couldn't believe what I was hearing.

"Pontiac Grand Prix?" I said.

"It was a Grand Prix," Devin said.

"Please, continue."

"I didn't think much about it at the time. The girls were staring back at me as I walked by the car. They were scared – that's for sure – but, they were really out of it, doped-up probably. This caught my attention, but knowing Gene, he always has young doper chicks around."

"I heard that before," I said, "then what?"

"I walked into David's garage and that's when I saw Cary Stayner."

"You saw Cary Stayner!" I said. "Are you sure?"

"I did," Devin said. "I had no idea who he was at the time. He just stood there. He looked like a bad-ass, that's for sure. It's when I saw the news, I recognized him."

"So, you were with Dykes and Stayner?"

"I sure as fuck was."

"Did Stayner say anything to you?"

"Nope," Devin said. "He just stood there and stared me down; gave me the fucking creeps."

"Remember the date?" I said.

"First week in March," Devin said.

"You sure," I said.

"My mom's birthday is on the second of March, I'm sure. It was the night after, when I met Stayner."

"Was there anyone else in the garage?"

"Nope; just me, Montessa, Gene Dykes, and Stayner."

"How long were you there?"

"About 15 minutes. I did a line and got the fuck out of there as soon as I could. I only bought a dime-bag. I had a bad feeling."

"What about the girls in the Pontiac? Did you recognize them?"

"When I walked by the car they were looking at me. No, I never saw them before."

"How young?"

"Young, maybe fifteen to seventeen. One had light brown hair and the other had dark hair."

Devin had put Stayner, Montessa, and Dykes together, and he saw two young girls in a red Pontiac Grand Prix. Along with the contents of the ditch, Devin was the witness that could get this case reopened.

"I told you I went to the ditch," I said.

"And, what did you think?" Devin said.

"I think you are what I have wished for," I said.

"All I will say is that you need to protect me . . . protect, my mother."

"That won't be a problem if you're exposed," I said.

"Promise?"

"I do," I said. "So, tell me more about the ditch in Salida."

"I went back to Montessa's house the next day. I asked him about Cary Stayner, and he said that he'd just met him. He said he didn't know much about him, but I guess Gene was friends with Stayner. I never saw Stayner again. I had no clue he was involved with the murders until it hit the news."

"And, the ditch?" I said.

"So, I was at David Montessa's and he asked me to get rid of some things. The jeep parts you saw, I put in there."

"So, the parts were from Dykes' Cherokee?"

"No, that's where everyone is wrong," Devin said. "The jeep belongs to David. Gene borrowed it to go to Mariposa."

"Is that right," I said.

"Sure is," Devin said. "Mariposa was what Gene told David. When David got his jeep back it was all fucked-up. The sides were dented and scratched to hell. Even the inside was tattered. The seats were torn and there was blood on them, on the dashboard too. There were a bunch of women's clothes inside. I knew something was up. David told me to come back with my truck and junk the shit."

"And you did," I said. "What were you thinking?"

"I was on dope, fuck-it. David gave me an eight-ball to bury the clothes and parts. I had no idea something was up."

"Fine, go on," I said.

"So, I came back that night and we loaded the truck. David had the entire jeep torn apart. I couldn't fucking believe it. The dash, seats, headliner, carpet, and all the instruments, were taken out. I was leaving and that's when Gene pulled up. I just kept going."

"Did he see you?" I said.

"He knows my truck," Devin said, "sure he did."

"Then you buried the stuff?" I said.

"I drove out to the ranch and unloaded everything; I buried it good. I didn't care what was going on at the time, but I regret it now."

Devin said he would testify witnessing Cary Stayner with Eugene Dykes - something the FBI needed and could never produce. Maybe they would be interested now. A whole other can of worms was about to be opened.

CHAPTER 47

January 17, 2004
San Francisco, California

"I COULDN'T HAVE MADE IT UP"

IT WAS AFTER midnight when we checked into a hotel on Van Ness Avenue, in San Francisco. Larry Murray's office was close by on Union Street, and Devin and I would be meeting Larry in the morning.

"We need to be up around eight," I said. "One more beer and then lights out."

"Sure," Devin said.

It was 7:00 a.m. the following morning, and Devin was up and having a cigarette. I had kidnapped Devin for safekeeping and a deposition. I was also close to getting his probation violated.

"Coffee is ready," Devin said.

"Thanks," I said. "And, Devin, don't worry about your probation officer. I'll have Larry call him."

Devin smiled in relief. "Cream?" he asked.

We arrived at Larry's office, just after nine. The interview room was ready with a small DVD camera on a tripod at the end of the long table.

"Are you going to be telling us the truth, Devin?" Larry asked.

"I have no reason to lie to you or anyone else," Devin said. "Is that camera on Mr. Murray?"

"It's been on," Larry said. "Please, call me Larry."

The interview lasted about a half-hour. Devin's statements on camera were the same as they were to me. Larry was impressed and thought we needed to take it to another level.

"Steve, you have a 400 pound gorilla on your back," Larry said. "Want me to make a call to the Attorney General's Office? You know we're old pals."

"No, not yet," I said.

"Well, your next best thing is to get some people to that ditch and go through everything. It's a crime scene. And, get Devin and his mother some protection, he'll need it."

"He needs to be in court tomorrow," I said, "but I don't want to risk losing him. He's too valuable. Can you take care of this?"

"Stan County?" Larry said.

I nodded.

"Greg is coming up from Fresno," Larry said, "I'll have him make an appearance for Devin. Don't worry about that, we got it. Get that ditch secure and then call me."

Back at the hotel room, I phoned Francis Carrington. He was very interested in the new discovery and said he'd leave for Modesto the following morning with Carole.

Devin and I left San Francisco around 10:00 that morning. He would be accompanying me to the "Carole Sund - Carrington Foundation" in Modesto. We arrived at the foundation a quarter after twelve.

"Don't slam the door, man," I said, to Devin.

"Sorry," Devin said, "I'm used to my truck."

"Are you ready?" I said.

"Let's do it."

Surprisingly, Devin had no apprehensions. I was anxious to bring him forward. As I led Devin through the door, the secretary greeted us. Then a familiar voice echoed from the hallway.

"Steve, so glad you made it," Kim said. "And this must be Devin."

It was Kim Peterson, Director of the foundation. I had not seen Kim for two years and she looked great. After a hug, she greeted Devin with a handshake.

"Follow me," Kim said. "Francis and Carole are here. Would you like a drink, some coffee or a Coke?"

"A coke," I said, "Devin?"

"That will be fine," Devin said, "thanks."

Kim pointed around the corner and Devin followed me into the conference room. I greeted the Carringtons and was introduced to Aaron Gallagher.

"Steve," Francis said, "Aaron is the Stanislaus County District Attorney Chief Investigator and one of our board members."

"And this is Devin," I said.

Francis opened the meeting. Devin responded politely and told his story. All eyes and ears were on my informant as his eyes canvassed the room. No one else said a word for 15 minutes. The room was quiet.

"That's quite a story, Devin," Aaron said.

"It's all true, sir," Devin said.

"Well, I think we should see this ditch," Francis said.

At about 1:15 that afternoon, we caravanned to Salida in two cars. I took Devin, and Aaron Gallagher drove the Carringtons and Kim Peterson. A couple of undercover units were in the area in case some dirt-bags took notice of the commotion. We parked alongside the ditch.

"This is it, Devin?" Aaron said.

"What do you want me to do?"

"Well, show us what you put in here," Aaron said. "I guess you should get in there."

Devin pointed and Aaron nodded yes. Devin turned to me.

"Go on," I said, "show us what you got."

Devin lifted the large piece of cardboard that covered some orange carpet. I looked at Aaron and he was watching Devin's every move. Devin pulled the carpet from the pile and I drug it up out of the hole. He then lifted one side of the seat and then the other. No doubt this was from a Jeep Cherokee.

"Looks like jeep parts alright," Aaron said, "where's the clothes?"

"Over here," Devin said.

I jumped in to help

"Oh my God," Kim said.

Aaron Gallagher turned to the Carringtons, "did any of this belong to Carole or the girls?"

The Carringtons' stood there frozen like statues.

"I don't know," Francis said finally.

Carole's eyes welled with tears. "Could be," she said," but there's no telling. I can't be certain."

"Hand Steve the rest, Devin," Aaron said.

We retrieved most of the clothing and placed it up top. The Carringtons, along with Kim, searched through the garments. No names on the tags or markings could be recognized. Shoes were also recovered with no personal markings. The sizes were close, but that

191

didn't do much for identifying who they belonged to.

"Is there anything else in there Devin?" Aaron asked.

"No, I think that's it," Devin said.

Now what? The jeep's carpet and bench seat were definitely close to the same year as David Montessa's jeep. The clothes were not confirmed as belonging to the women, but I'll bet they were. This was not a coincidence. As some of us meandered around the ditch, I spotted something that made me take a closer look.

"Excuse me," I said, as I walked between Kim and Aaron.

I stepped into the ditch and retrieved a gift bag with hearts, a "Valentine's" bag. My heart stopped, and so did everyone else's as I walked out holding the bag. The abduction had occurred on February 15, 1999, Valentine's weekend.

I felt like I was going to drop to my knees. The car parts, the clothes, and a witness that put Cary Stayner and Eugene Dykes together, and now a Valentine's bag. If this wasn't it, nothing was. Using my knife, I handed the bag to Aaron Gallagher, and his face was stone.

"Aaron, we need to forensic this hole in the ground now," I said.

Aaron said nothing as he stared at the Valentine's bag.

"Aaron," Francis said.

The implications were sinking in to everyone. "Oh yes, I need to make a call," Aaron said.

The D.A. investigator walked away punching numbers into his cell phone. A few minutes later he walked up to Francis, and I.

"We have a team coming out," Aaron said.

"Good," Francis said.

"I want the bag checked-out and this ditch gone through," Aaron said. "Let's back off and leave things be."

Francis looked at me and I nodded. I put my arm over Devin's shoulders.

"Thanks," I said quietly.

We all felt a heavy silence that fell like a shroud over the place.

This place was a sanctuary that needed to be cleansed. The crime scene was old, and there was a lot of doubt that any decent physical evidence would be found, but it was worth a shot and needed to be done. Aaron was looking at the bag when I approached.

"Devin," I said, "wait by the car."

"I have to ask you, Steve," Aaron said, "how did you come upon

192

Paul Candler?"

"I had him out on bond and he skipped," I said.

"What led you to him, how did you find him in Alabama? I want to know what made you think he was involved."

I gave Aaron Gallagher the dime store version.

"Wow! " Aaron said. "Candler was a tough bounty for you."

"Paul Candler was the *Ultimate Prey.*"

"You may not realize this," Aaron said, "I was following your moves with Paul Candler from the time you landed in Alabama, to the arrest. I can tell you this, Dykes and Larwick are involved and we can't do much with them. I had their files on my desk for three years. I still have Paul Candler's on my desk."

That was all I needed to hear. . .

Map of 5 Victims' Locations & Routes the Killers' Drove

Complete Map

Yosemite National Park

4

120

Mt. Reba Ski Resort

207

Larwick's prior
Residence

Dr. Wong

Yosemite
Valley

Bear Valley

Dorrington   Long Barn   Wheeler Rd.

120

Candler's
prior
Residence   Twain Harte   Carole Sund
Silvina Pelosso

Arnold

Murphys   Buck Meadows

140

4   108   Foresta

Joie Armstrong

Angels
Camp   El Portal   Cedar
Lodge

Groveland

Sonora   Stayner's
Residence

Melones   Jamestown

49   120

Chinese
Camp   Candler's
Residence   Briceburg

Lake Don Pedro   Grizzly Rd.

108   Moccasin

Juli Sund

49

Coulterville   140

Mariposa
Airport

Murder Victims' Locations

Map is not to Scale   Mt. Bullion   Mariposa

Drawn by Stephen M. Sanzeri   49

194

EPILOGUE

The Valentine's bag was traced to a manufacturer out of New Hampshire. It was made between 1996 and 1999, and sold all over the United States. No prints were recovered from the bag. As for the ditch and its contents, all forensic testing came up negative for physical evidence; no prints, hair, blood, DNA, etc.

The impounded jeep of David Montessa was gone over again. The "white coats" couldn't verify that the carpet and seat from the ditch, originally belonged to David's jeep.

And most upsetting was the fact that investigators left Devin alone. Besides Rhonda Dunn, he was the only witness willing to come forward that placed Cary Stayner with Eugene Dykes. After all this, and the case gained zero momentum.

There was not much more I could do. I knew it was finally over for me.

I have never been involved in such an important and personal investigation; to be in a position that made a dramatic difference in others' lives as well as my own.

Something happened to me that day, looking over that ditch in Salida. Sure, we couldn't wrap the case up neatly and tie it with a bow. The evidence was old and inconclusive. Law enforcement didn't want to mess with the case anymore, and everyone was torn up and burned out, especially the families.

But, seeing that Valentine's Day bag lying in the dirt is a picture that I will never forget. And, like a Valentine, part of my own heart will remain with the memory of those innocent women and their families for the rest of my life.

Present Day:

I received the phone call around 11:50, Tuesday evening. I didn't recognize the phone number but I answered. It was August 22, 2012.

It was Nancy Lawson's mother, whom I never spoken to. "Nancy committed suicide," she told me.

I reacted with the standard, "I am so sorry." And then, I couldn't speak or move. I didn't cry. I had no emotions or thoughts.

I felt a flood of guilt like warm blood rushing through my body. .I knew why Nancy did this.

Her mother then said that Nancy left three notes and one was for me. "Tell Steve, I love him and make sure he knows."

I was somber, as if I just died. Nothing like this had ever happened to me.

I had just spoken with Nancy the prior Wednesday, after she read the book. She was excited and very happy with the way I wrote her story; a story that a lot of people were skeptical about. But, Nancy said that I left something out, something very important.

She told me that Ricardo actually did see Juli Sund in Mick Larwick's garage. "He told me he didn't want to be a witness and lied to you. He was sure it was Juli. Why do you think he was so nervous? Why do think he didn't want me in the van while he was talking to you guys? Fuck, Steve, the FBI was buying him lunch and he still didn't tell them. I would have called him on it," Nancy said.

I wasn't aware of this until now. Why did she wait so many years to tell me? Either way, Nancy guided me into the abyss of the central valley. I understood Nancy and she did great. But, was she holding secrets I needed for the case?

Nancy Lawson carried the murders of Carole, Juli and Silvina, like a mother who had lost a child. Nancy was in fact, a rape victim of Eugene Dykes and that was the link in the chain she couldn't break. For 12 years, Nancy lived her own nightmare while trying to help solve a case that was wronged from the beginning.

A loving and beautiful woman, I already miss her late night phone calls telling me to talk to this guy or that girl. Hell, I yelled at her at times, "Let it fucking go, Nancy. Move on with your life." She couldn't.

Nancy's death is collateral damage from this case. A case that happened over a decade ago.

Do I have any guilt? Absolutely. How can I not feel something? But my guilt is only a very small part of the Love I have for Nancy. She didn't close her final chapter in vain. Nancy wanted me to tell her story. I just didn't expect such a sad and tragic ending.

Nancy, I will never forget you...

~ *The End* ~

CHRONOLOGY OF
THE YOSEMITE CASE AND INVESTIGATION

February 14, 1999 - Carole Sund, Juli Sund and Silvina Pelosso drive to El Portal, California, and check into room 509 at the Cedar Lodge. It's Valentine's Day.

February 15, 1999 - The trio visits Yosemite, returning in the late afternoon to have dinner at the Cedar Lodge restaurant.

February 17, 1999 - Jens Sund reports his wife, daughter and Silvina, missing the day after they miss a rendezvous at SFO.

February 18, 1999 - Mariposa County Sheriff's Department starts their search for Carole, Juli and Silvina, and the red Pontiac rental car. It is initially believed they were in an accident and went over a cliff.

February 19, 1999 - Doctor Katherine Wong is reported missing while skiing at Mr. Reba Ski Resort in Bear Valley, Alpine County, California. Dr. Wong is not found after a five days search.

February 19, 1999 - Carole Sund's wallet insert is found by a pedestrian at the intersection of Briggsmore Ave. and Tully Road in Modesto, California.

February 20, 1999 - Francis and Carole Carrington offer a $250,000.00 reward for information leading to the girls' safe return.

February 20, 1999 - A fire occurs at 55784 Grizzly Road, in Moccasin; Candler's address. His sister owns the home. Fire is of unknown origin. The kitchen area and attached garage wall are damaged.

February 20, 1999 - Modesto, California, Rick and I are on a bounty. I read about the disappearance of Doctor Wong. On the way

197

home, Candler phones me and admits that he started a fire, and the cops were after him.

February 22, 1999 - The Sacramento FBI joins the investigation. Agent Jeff Rinek is designated as the FBI's lead investigator. A month later, Special Agent in Charge, James Maddock, abruptly removes Agent Rinek from the case. Agent Nick Rossi becomes the lead investigator.

March 3, 1999 - Devin meets Cary Stayner for the first and last time. Eugene Dykes is also present in David Montessa's garage. Devin notices a red Pontiac Grand Prix parked in front. Two teenage girls are in the car and appear doped-up.

March 5, 1999 - Billy Joe Strange is arrested in Mariposa County for a parole violation. He was the first suspect arrested.

March 5, 1999 - Eugene "Rufus" Dykes is arrested on a parole violation in Modesto after a two and a half hour standoff.

March 6, 1999 - Investigators question Cedar Lodge handyman Cary Stayner, but are unable to link Stayner to the missing women.

March 9, 1999 - Michael "Mick" Larwick fails to appear in Tuolumne County Superior Court on charges of methamphetamine possession and a bench warrant is issued. Michael Larwick is the half-brother of Eugene Dykes.

March 14, 1999 - The FBI arrests Darrell Stephens as a possible suspect.

March 15, 1999 - Paul Candler Jr. fails to appear in court on my bond and a bench warrant is issued.

March 18, 1999 - Michael Larwick is arrested after a 14-hour standoff, after shooting Modesto Police Officer Steve Silva.

March 18, 1999 - Carole Sund's burned rental car is found on Wheeler Road off Highway 108 in Long Barn, Tuolumne County.

The bodies of Carole Sund and Silvina Pelosso are identified four days later. Long Barn is Michael Larwick's child hood hometown.

March 19, 1999 - I receive the bail forfeiture for Paul Candler Jr.

March 25, 1999 - Juli Sund's body is located by law enforcement below the Highway 49 lookout in Moccasin, a few yards above Lake Don Pedro.

March 26, 1999 - The FBI arrests Johnny Nolan Jr., Larry Utley and Jeffery Wayne Keeney as suspects in the Yosemite case. The FBI labels the investigation as, "Tour-Nap."

March 27, 1999 - I start the bounty hunt for Candler and confirm the distances between Juli Sund's body and Candler's residence; only 2 miles by road or about a quarter mile across Lake Don Pedro by boat.

March 28, 1999 - The FBI reveals that a loose knit group of meth users is now the focus of their investigation.

April 1, 1999 - Candler closes his Post Office box in Moccasin, California.

April 6, 1999 - Terry Ray, a material witness in the Yosemite case, is found drowned in the Stanislaus River in the Modesto area.

April 7, 1999 - The Federal Grand Jury in Fresno begins their investigation. They focus on suspects' Michael Larwick and Eugene Dykes, as well as others.

May 27, 1999 - I forwarded my first report to the FBI Task Force in Sonora.

June 4, 1999 - Barbara's step daughter, Anne, calls and tells me that Barbara and Paul are in Alabama. Anne gives me a good phone number.

June 5, 1999 - Rick and I fly to Birmingham, Alabama, after confirming that Barbara Dobbins is employed as a mobile home sales person in Sumiton, Alabama.

June 6, 1999 - The FBI arrests Kenneth "Soldier" Stewart.

June 7, 1999 - Rick and I arrest Paul Candler in Fultondale, Alabama, after a short standoff and fight. Birmingham FBI interviews Candler the same day regarding the Yosemite homicides.

June 8, 1999 - The decomposed and dismembered body of Dr. Katherine Wong is discovered at Mt. Reba Ski Resort. It's ironic that her body was found the day after we arrest Paul Candler. It appears that Candler told the FBI where the doctor's body was located. Candler had a prior address in Arnold, 30 miles west of Mt. Reba. Barbara Dobbins worked at El Dorado Savings in Arnold.

June 27, 1999 - Reporter Mike Mooney, interviews a witness in the Yosemite case named Rhonda Dunn.

July 22, 1999 - Naturalist Joie Armstrong, 26, is found decapitated near her remote cabin. The FBI says there is no connection to the Sund-Pelosso slayings and maintains that key suspects in that case are behind bars on unrelated charges.

July 22, 1999 - Law enforcement immediately questions Cary Stayner about the disappearance of Joie Armstrong.

July 23, 1999 - Cary Stayner, questioned earlier in the case, fails to show up for work at the Cedar Lodge. The FBI begins a search.

July 24, 1999 - Cary Stayner is taken into custody at Laguna Del Sol, a nudist colony in Winton, California. FBI Agent Jeff Rinek makes the arrest. Stayner confesses to all four murders.

July 25, 1999 - A Federal Magistrate in Fresno, charges Cary Stayner with the murder of Joie Armstrong.

July 25, 1999 - The FBI announces there is information linking Cary Stayner to the murders of Carol, Juli and Silvina. The FBI charges Stayner with the murder of Ms. Armstrong.

July 26, 1999 - Stayner tells reporter Ted Rowlands, in a jailhouse interview that he alone killed all four women and expects to plead guilty. Stayner said he wants a TV movie just like his brother Steven.

August 6, 1999 - Stayner pleads innocent in federal court to Joie Armstrong's murder.

September 22, 1999 - Stayner pleads innocent to additional charges of trying to sexually assault and kidnap Joie Armstrong.

September 30, 1999 - Tuolumne County District Attorney, Nina Deane, resigns six months into her second elected term citing a desire to "go sailing" with her husband.

October 20, 1999 - The Mariposa County District Attorney charges Stayner with capital murder in the slayings of Carole Sund, Juli Sund and Silvina Pelosso.

February 12, 2000 - Paul Candler attacks Rick Janes at the Shell gas station in Arnold. Calaveras County Sheriff's Office covers it up and no charges are filed on Candler.

November 30, 2000 - Cary Stayner pleads guilty in Federal Court to the murder of Joie Armstrong. In exchange prosecutors will not seek the death penalty.

June 3, 2000 - Jury in Merced, California, found Paul Candler Jr. guilty of the continuous sexual molestation of a 12-year-old girl. He was sentenced to 17-years in Tehachapi State Prison.

July 13, 2000 - I met with former Alpine County Deputy "Phil," who investigated the disappearance and death of Dr. Wong. Phil knows it's a homicide.

March 27, 2001 - I contacted Zach Zwerdling, attorney for the Sund family. He welcomed my information because he was also skeptical about Cary Stayner as the lone killer. He suggests I speak to Rhonda Dunn. I contact Rhonda Dunn, who describes a man very similar to Paul Candler.

April 5, 2001 - From the photo lineup I sent, Rhonda Dunn identifies Candler as one of the people with Cary Stayner at the Cedar Lodge.

April 30, 2001 - I meet with Orb Hatton and discover that Orb is the reason I posted bail for Candler. Orb believes he was the target of a "hit for hire," with Candler as the hit man. Orb worked undercover to infiltrate the Mariposa County drug trade in the mid 1980's. He was also looking into Deputy Van Meter's death.

August 13, 2001 - I met with the Carringtons for the first time in Eureka. I become the investigator for the family.

August 15, 2001 - My first meeting with Nancy Lawson in Modesto.

September 1, 2001 - Francis Carrington receives a phone call from an anonymous law enforcement source stating that Paul Candler Jr. is probably involved with the Yosemite murders.

September 2, 2001 - Francis Carrington receives a phone call from Mariposa Deputy District Attorney, Kim Fletcher. She tells Mr. Carrington that I'm an asshole and too take me off the case.

September 4, 2001 - I receive a call from Mariposa County Detective Kathy Sarno. She requests an interview.

September 6, 2001 - Rick and I meet with Detective Sarno at my office.

September 30, 2001 - The Modesto Bee runs the first story of my investigation on the front page. I had updated reporter Mike Mooney, after the meeting with Detective Sarno.

December 9, 2001 - I interview Diane Gibson regarding information she had on Eugene Dykes, Michael Larwick, and a witness named, Rick Stiles. Ms. Gibson said that Stiles was at a party when Dykes and Larwick had Juli Sund enslaved. I videotaped the interview. (*Not in the book*)

February 14, 2002 - Valentine's Day, and a day away from the third anniversary of the murders. Mike Mooney wrote a second story, this time regarding Stayner's defense and naming the original suspects, with Paul Candler as the number-one guy to look at.

February 18, 2002 - The Modesto Bee revised the February 14, story and ran it again.

February 22, 2002 - Rick Stiles phones and tells me he was brought before the Grand Jury as a witness. He said he lied on purpose. With his permission, I tapped our conversation. Stiles didn't deny seeing Juli. (*Not in the book*)

February 25, 2002 - I receive a phone call from FBI Agent, Rossi. We discuss the case.

March 4, 2002 - Informant, Nancy Lawson, sets a meeting with Ricardo, a friend of Eugene Dykes and Michael Larwick's. Ricardo was a material witness and interviewed by the FBI after he saw a girl in Larwick's garage who resembled Juli Sund. Rick and I believe it was Juli. Ricardo said it wasn't Juli.

May 7, 2002 - My first conversation with FBI Agent Nick Rossi.

July 15, 2002 - The State's capital murder trial against Cary Stayner begins in Superior Court, in Santa Clara County. Judge Thomas Hastings presides.

July 17, 2002 - I meet with Rhonda Dunn, a second time. Rhonda Identifies Eugene Dykes from an older newspaper photograph. Rhonda recognizes Dykes from the Cedar Lodge with Cary Stayner and Paul Candler.

August 11, 2002 - Agent Rossi phones and I play the recording of Rick Stiles.

August 12, 2002 - Eugene Dykes appears in Superior Court as a witness in Cary Stayner's trial. Dykes exercises his Fifth Amendment Right and keeps his mouth shut.

August 12, 2002 - Agent Rossi requests that I write a report for the FBI, in preparation of the other suspects being subpoenaed in Stayner's trial.

August 26, 2002 - Cary Stayner is found guilty of killing Carole Sund, Juli Sund and Silvina Pelosso.

September 17, 2002 - The Jury finds Cary Stayner sane when he committed the homicides.

December 12, 2002 - Cary Stayner is sentenced to death. I receive this information over the radio while on a bounty in Denver, Colorado. I was living in San Diego at this time.

March 7, 2003 - Sacramento television station KOVR (CBS) ran a special on the Yosemite Sightseer Case. For the first time in two years, Francis and Carole Carrington spoke publicly about others involved. FBI's Nick Rossi was also interviewed and stuck to his guns. "Unless somebody has evidence to implicate others, the FBI will do nothing."

March 9, 2003 - This is the second year that I attend the Carole Sund / Carrington Memorial Reward Foundation's annual "Vigil of Hope," in Modesto. I meet with Chandra Levy's parents.

January 13, 2004 - Nancy Lawson calls and begs me to meet with an informant. I am living in San Diego.

January 15, 2004 - I meet with the informant, Devin, for the first time at the mall in Modesto. Devin escorts Nancy to the ditch in Salida, late that evening. Early morning, Devin is arrested on a warrant for missing a drug class.

January 16, 2004 - I bail Devin out of Stanislaus County Jail and we meet.

January 17, 2004 - Devin sits down for a videotaped interview with Attorney Larry Murray, in San Francisco. Devin tells the full story, placing Eugene Dykes and Cary Stayner together in Montessa's garage. He tells about seeing the red Pontiac and how he tossed the car parts and clothing into the ditch in Salida.

January 18, 2004 - Devin escorts the Carringtons, Kim Peterson, Aaron Gallagher, and me to the ditch in Salida. I discover the Valentine's gift bag.

------------------ACKNOWLEDGMENTS------------------

To Francis and Carole Carrington, who gave me their blessing and the chance to investigate and help with this case. Their incredible strength kept me going throughout this challenging task and taught me a lot about myself.

To Kim Peterson, Director of the Carole Sund/Carrington Memorial Reward Foundation, who assisted me with the investigation and supported my objective.

To my cop buddies, John Kiramis, Rich Camps, Ron Cloward, Skip Bernasconi and Tom Donohue, for letting me chew on their ears during my times of frustration and giving me guidance.

Mike Mooney. Thanks for taking an interest and believing in my investigation. You helped me to tell the real story.

To my mother Jo Anne, who supported every endeavor I've ever accomplished and failed. I Love you mom, rest in peace.

To my father, you taught me never to give up and to be tough. I love you dad. RIP.

Attorney Larry Murray, who stood behind and bailed me out of trouble, even though you warned me on more than one occasion not to stick my nose in it.

Rick Janes, the best partner I ever had. I wouldn't have caught most of the bail jumpers without you. And to his wife Kathy, who assisted and kept us laughing when times were gloomy.

My good friend Fred Baker. You read the very first draft 10 years ago while we were visiting Mexico. Thanks for pushing me to finish this story.

Jack "Coach" Burgett, all I can say is . . . thanks for everything.

Mimi Baker, you have read everything I've written. Your expertise as a script supervisor has been a true gift from a great friend.

Molly Giles, thank you for reading the manuscript. Your handwritten note was very inspirational.

Marlene Aldelstein, my very first editor. You said I had two books and that's exactly what has happened. Your advice was Golden.

Bruce Porter, thank you for reading my manuscript while on vacation. I appreciate your positive comments early on.

Dave Rasmussen, I owe you a debt of gratitude for sending my mess of a manuscript to Bruce Porter.

Dennis McDougal, thank you for enlightening me with confidential information and writing the very first book about the case.

Berni Kunz, thanks for your support over the years and believing in this project.

Skip, my brother, you have survived huge obstacles, where most folks, including myself, may have tossed in the towel. Your strength of survival was inspirational guidance for me to complete this story.

Suza Lambert Bowser, my lovely editor. Thank you.

To my precious "Froggy." You gave me the inspiration to keep this investigation going when I wanted to quit. During those uncertain nights away from home, thoughts would cross my mind of us never seeing each other again. But you gave me the strength to make it home safely. You're the reason I wrote this story; therefore I also dedicate this book to you, Love Daddy.

A contribution from the royalties will be made to the

Carole Sund/Carrington Memorial Reward Fund

Contributions may be sent to:

Carole Sund/Carrington Memorial Reward Foundation
1508 Coffee Road, Suite H
Modesto, CA 95350

A contribution from the royalties will also be made to the

Joie Ruth Armstrong Memorial Fund
For Youth Educational Programs

Contributions may be sent to:
Joie Armstrong Memorial Fund
c/o Yosemite National Institutes
GGNRA, Building 1055
Sausalito, CA 94965

If you liked this book, you'll certainly enjoy

IT'S ONLY A BUSINESS

"True Stories Of A Modern Day Bounty Hunter"

by

Stephen M. Sanzeri

Look for it – **Fall, 2012**

ISBN **978-0-9859144-2-4**

Made in the USA
Las Vegas, NV
02 December 2023